Launching the Writing Workshop

Lucy Calkins and Amanda Hartman

Photography by Peter Cunningham

HEINEMANN ◆ PORTSMOUTH, NH

This book is dedicated to Tameem, may you always find that the hard work of writing is a joy—especially when it is shared.

Heinemann
361 Hanover Street
Portsmouth, NH 03801–3912
www.heinemann.com

Offices and agents throughout the world

The authors and publisher wish to thank those who have generously given permission to reprint borrowed material:

Creak! Said the Bed by Phyllis Root. Text copyright © 2010 Phyllis Root. Illustrations copyright © 2010 Regan Dunnick. Reproduced by permission of the publisher, Candlewick Press, Somerville, MA.

Cataloging-in-Publication data is on file with the Library of Congress.

ISBN-13: 978-0-325-04720-1

Production: Elizabeth Valway, David Stirling, and Abigail Heim
Cover and interior designs: Jenny Jensen Greenleaf
Series includes photographs by Peter Cunningham, Nadine Baldasare, and Elizabeth Dunford
Composition: Publishers' Design and Production Services, Inc.
Manufacturing: Steve Bernier

Printed in the United States of America on acid-free paper
21 20 19 18 17 VP 2 3 4 5 6

Acknowledgments

THIS BOOK WAS A BIG RESPONSIBILITY. It was the first in the new series to be written, and we knew from the success of the previous series that it will probably reach into the classrooms of half the schools in this country and in thousands overseas. We asked ourselves, how do we help kindergarten teachers feel at home starting the teaching of writing from the very first moment of kindergarten? And how do we create minilessons and write about conferring and small groups in ways that far outstrip anything that was done in the original beautiful series?

The two of us are especially grateful to each other—and to that magic that happens when one plus one is far greater than two. We had a blast writing this book, although it took us ten times longer than we anticipated.

The book not only took us longer than we dreamt possible, but it also brought a larger community of supporters together than we had imagined. In the end, the insights and ideas in this book come not just from the two of us, but also from brilliant, amazing Kate Montgomery, who especially played a major role in the last third of the book. Julia Mooney was a source of great support and wisdom, and we thank her as well.

The ideas in this book have emerged from work in thousands of kindergarten classrooms in every state of the U.S. and many nations—and we are grateful to those who have shared that work with us: Shanna, Christine, Natalie, Lauren, Monique, Celena, Rebecca, Lindsay, Rachel, Katie, Sadia, Marjorie, Ellen, Beth, Enid, Sarah, Elizabeth, Brianna, and Ryan. The staff development and classroom-based research is only possible because of work that the Teachers College Reading and Writing Project (TCRWP) leaders do, and we are grateful to Laurie Pessah, Mary Ehrenworth, and Kathleen Tolan for helping us lead the organization.

Thank you to the office staff at the TCRWP for all their attention and hard work, and especially to Kalei Sabaratnam, who helped to organize the student work featured in this book.

We would also like to thank the Heinemann team, and especially Felicia O'Brien for her attention to detail, Stephanie Parsons for ferreting out problems that we needed to address, and Abby Heim for leading every little bit of production, and doing so with grace, class, and impeccable standards.

Lastly, our thanks go to the schools that have worked with us, that have helped us to shape our ideas and to show us what is possible in kindergarten. Special thanks to Adele Schroeder and Kristi Mraz at PS 59 in Manhattan and to Anthony Inzcrillo, Karen Gibbons, Kristen Puleio, and Karen Bruno at PS 199 in Queens. Your schools and classrooms have been inspirations to us and to educators from across the world. Thank you for showing us, again and again, what it means to create joyful, innovative, and rigorous kindergarten classrooms.

The class described in this unit is a composite class, with children and partnerships of children gleaned from classrooms in very different contexts, then put together here. We wrote the units this way to bring you both a wide array of wonderful, quirky, various children and also to illustrate for you the predictable (and unpredictable) situations and responses this unit has created in classrooms across the nation and world.

—Lucy and Amanda

Contents

BEND III   Writing Stories

BEND IV   Preparing for Publication

 Registration instructions to access the digital resources that accompany this book may be found on p. ix.

Welcome to the Unit

THE BEGINNING OF KINDERGARTEN is a time of new possibilities. Kindergartners enter school ready to read and write like big kids, to learn alongside classmates, and to take the world by storm. This first unit of study, *Launching the Writing Workshop*, capitalizes on that excitement and channels it into writing all-about books and stories. Notice, then, that although most books in this series are about a particular kind of writing—information, narrative, or opinion writing, this book straddles two kinds of writing and focuses especially on launching the writing workshop and launching kids into the identity and work of being writers.

We hope the unit helps you begin your writing workshop at the very start of the year because we know that if the writing workshop becomes part of your everyday routine, the results will take your breath away. Time and again, teachers have said to us, "If I hadn't seen it with my own eyes, I would never have believed that my kindergartners could do so much—and with such joy!"

The most important thing we can say about September in the kindergarten writing workshop is this: don't wait! It is tempting to think that children need to know the alphabet before you launch the writing workshop or that they need to be socialized into the rhythms of the school day before you start this teaching. It is not so. You can start on Day One. Writing workshop is made-to-order for the start of kindergarten.

We encourage you to take the brave step of gathering children on the first day of school and inviting them to live like writers. That may seem crazy, given that you know many of your children don't know their letters and sounds yet. But remember, if you line three chairs up and invite kindergartners to climb aboard your train, they'll have no hesitation! If you pass the broom to a child and ask him to help you sweep, chances are good that he'll go at it with eagerness—whether or not he has any clue what to do with that broom! Your children have no problem pretending to be queens and kings, deep sea

divers, and astronauts. So the truth is that children find it utterly reasonable to be given paper and some marker pens and to be invited to make an all-about book.

Some children will draw rather than write sentences. However, you'll find that, with help, a surprising number of children can write some letters alongside their drawings. In *Kindergarten Literacy*, Anne McGill Franzen reminds us of the research from the Early Childhood Longitudinal Study (ECLS-K) that The National Center for Education Statistics collected and analyzed. According to this data, two-thirds of kindergarten children come to school knowing the alphabet. Depending on the context in which you teach, you may well have many children who are already able to write conventionally. No matter where your students are developmentally, this unit will help them build the foundational skills they need. Those skills are increasingly important in this era of world-class standards.

To be a kindergarten teacher now is to be living in an age of change. Any kindergarten teacher will tell you, it is complicated. On the one hand, kindergarten is only offered half-day in many schools and is not mandatory in many cities and states. Complaints from parents, and occasionally the media, charge that kindergarten is becoming too academic and that childhood must be safeguarded. On the other hand, children entering first grade not knowing how to read are considered "at risk" or "behind," and in many ways they are. This is an issue of equity. While in one community, nearly all children attend kindergarten and are engaged in rich literacy experiences with books and writing, drawing and storytelling—in another community, kindergarten isn't even available in the public schools. For decades kindergarten teachers have struggled with how much to expect, academically, from their pint-sized scholars if they aren't even required, officially, to be in school at all.

Although primary teachers debate whether it is helpful for kindergarten to be focused on academics rather than play, most state standards make it clear that five-year-olds need time to learn to write. Standards state that young children deserve the opportunity and experience of writing at least three types of text: stories, opinions, and information texts. These standards situate kindergarten as an important starting point for children's lifelong learning as writers. We agree with this position, although we celebrate the fact that embracing the kindergarten writing workshop does not mean refuting the developmentally appropriate playful kindergarten—far from it!

This unit launches work for children to write both information books and true stories—writing "as best they can." In the first half of the unit, children learn how to write informative/explanatory texts—texts that teach readers information about which the children are experts. Then, in the second half of the unit, they learn how to write and record personal narratives. They also are introduced to very early versions of both revision and editing.

Meanwhile, children will learn also what it means to be part of a writing workshop. After all, minilessons and conferences are not just methods of teaching; they are also methods of learning. Your children will learn the roles they are to play in all the various parts of a writing workshop. As part of this, they will learn how to work with each other as partners—planning together, sharing drafts, giving each other help. As children do this work together, they'll work with reading as well as writing standards. They will learn to ask and answer questions about information texts, and they'll begin to develop ideas about authors, illustrators, and genre.

OVERVIEW OF THE UNIT

This unit is divided into four bends in the road—four sections. During the first bend of the unit, your aim will be to introduce youngsters to the writing workshop. "You are an author," you'll say, and you'll help youngsters understand how to think up a topic, to draw it, and then to do their best approximation of writing. At the start of the unit, you'll expect youngsters to make a quick piece of writing and then announce, "I'm done!" Soon, then, you'll teach children to linger longer and invest more in a piece of writing—thus launching an elementary school career of learning to elaborate! You'll also teach youngsters how to go from finishing one piece to starting another and to do this with some independence.

One of the most important messages you can possibly teach is that writers start with something to say and then do everything they can to put that meaning onto the page. The writing process starts with a writer having content, an image, and then drawing representationally to put that meaning onto the page. The writer then looks at what's on the page, comparing that with his or her mental image—the intended meaning—asking, "What have I left out? What should I add?"

In no time, children will use letters as well as pictures to represent meaning. Your youngsters will develop phonemic awareness as they stretch out, listen to, distinguish, and record the sounds in a word. They will learn to use tools to help them with this writing, starting with a name chart to help them record letters and words on a page.

The second bend in the road of the unit is titled "Writing Teaching Books." During this portion of the unit, children learn that they can reread what they have written, realize they have more to say, then staple on more pages to make a homemade book. The thrill of stapling can lure youngsters to add on, putting more information into their information books. Of course, in just a few days, children will begin approaching their writing with the intention to say more from the start. Children will plan across the pages of their booklets and will elaborate more. You'll channel children's eagerness to fill up all the pages in their books into a willingness to label more of their pictures, to represent more sounds in a word, and to make two-word labels. These labels will often include high-frequency words (such as *the*) or descriptive words (such a *big*).

Things change dramatically in the third portion of the unit, "Writing Stories." Up until now, children will have learned that they can write to teach people all about whatever they know. Now, they learn that they can also write to capture true stories from their lives. You'll encourage children to put the small episodes of their lives onto the page. They will draw what happened first, then touch the page and tell the story, and then they will write the story of that one time. Although the stories you demonstrate will be what this series refers to as "Small Moment stories" of very focused episodes, the important thing in this unit is not to teach children that their stories need to be focused; instead, it is to teach them that they can take the things they do and tell the story of those events in homemade books. Children will learn that to write true stories, writers think about what happened and then draw and write what happened first, then turn the page and tell what happened next and then next. Your children will be eager to learn the tricks of the trade, so you'll teach some early lessons in narrative craft.

In the last bend of the unit, your children will select a few stories to publish and will learn to revise and edit as they make those stories the best they can be. To do this, you'll introduce children to the checklists that will undergird every unit of study. With guidance from the checklist and from you, children will make their best writing better. They'll add details to their writing and they'll fix up spellings, getting more sounds into their words. Then, to culminate the unit, students will celebrate by reading selections from their writing to the circle of their classmates.

ASSESSMENT

We recommend that you start each school year, K–5, by devoting one writing workshop to having students write a short, timed, on-demand piece that you'll use for assessment for each of the three types of writing. That is, we suggest that you ask children to write their best narrative on one day, their best information writing on another day, and their best opinion writing on a third day.

We're aware that this probably sounds a bit outlandish. "Welcome to kindergarten. Let me test you. And furthermore, let me test you in something you don't begin to know how to do (nor should you)." But here is the thing: thousands and thousands of teachers have done as we are suggesting and found this to be extraordinarily powerful—so don't dismiss the idea altogether.

Why has this been powerful? First, when you conduct this assessment, you come to realize that it's simply not the case that at the start of the year, kindergartners are all at the starting gate. From the start, there will be vast differences in your children's understandings of written language, and those differences will be immediately apparent. Then, too, capturing what youngsters know and can do at the very start of the year provides you with a dramatic and accessible way to be able to eventually demonstrate your students' progress. If you collect baseline data, then on Parent's Night you'll be able to say, "This is what your child came to school doing as a writer, and now this is his latest work." Of course, this means not only that you'll have bragging rights over your children's progress; it also means you will have a way to measure the effectiveness of your teaching.

The details of the on-demand assessment, including the specific prompts, are laid out in the book in this series entitled *Writing Pathways: Performance Assessments and Learning Progressions, K–5*. For information writing, the prompt to the children begins, "Think of a topic that you've studied or that you know a lot about." You'll want to let your youngsters know that they can use the whole writing workshop (forty-five minutes of actual writing time, plus whatever talking you do) to write the best they can and to fill their pages with as much information as they can teach.

For the narrative on-demand writing, the prompt begins, "I'm really eager to understand what you can do as writers of narratives, of stories, so today, will you please write the best personal narrative, the best Small Moment story that you can write?" This unit will further students' work in both information and narrative writing, so it is best for you to collect on-demand writing in at least these two types of writing even if you decide not to collect opinion writing at this point.

Because the work that your children produce will end up being part of a K–5 progression, we hope that you are willing to give children some pointers that will not mean anything to most of them yet. In an assessment, it is important that the conditions are kept the same, when possible, so that results can be compared. So although the pointers are not apt to mean anything to five-year-olds, we want to give these prompts now so that everyone, K–5, is given the same prompt, the same opportunities. In any case, the pointers for information writing include, "Remember to name what topic you will teach about, try to give information to help readers learn a lot about your topic, and make an ending for your teaching book. Use pictures and words to help you write." The pointers for narrative writing, on the other hand, include, "Make a beginning for your story, show what happened, use details, and make an ending for your story."

As children are drawing and writing their on-demand tasks for assessment, you will want to move quickly among them, asking them to tell you what they are writing and then recording verbatim what they say so that you are essentially taking down a dictation. Usually teachers record the youngster's intended message on a Post-it® that they later stick onto the back of the writing. Later, when you collect students' writing and try to understand whether their spelling was somewhat phonetic, for example, you'll find that the records of what the writers intended to say will help you decipher what they wrote and what the logic was that informed their writing.

You may want to duplicate your students' on-demand writing so that they can keep copies of their work inside their writing folders (and you keep a copy as well in your records). These will serve as models of what children are able to do at the very start of the year. Children can then strive to do even better as the unit and the year progress—and of course, their skills will grow in leaps and bounds this first year. Eventually, you and your students, and their parents, too, will see evidence of that growth by comparing later work with this initial work.

You will use your copies of these initial on-demand pieces to assess where each of your students fall in both the narrative and the information K–5 learning progressions and, especially, to learn where the majority of children fall so that you can plan your upcoming unit of study with that data in mind. Whereas in most grades, you'll expect that children's work at the start of the year will reach and illustrate the standards for the preceding year, our assessment system does not provide a checklist for (or benchmark texts for) prekindergarten. You should not expect that at the start of the year your children are anywhere close to performing at kindergarten levels. Those levels are for end-of-the-year expectations.

Still, examining the students' on-demand work will help you know a bit about what they bring to the unit. It will be significant for you to note whether children are entering the unit with knowledge of letters and sounds. If this is the case, you'll be more apt to anticipate that from the start, some of them will be writing on paper with lines for their sentences (as well as space for labeled drawings). It will also be interesting to see whether your children, at the start of kindergarten, have any sense that the sort of work they produce when asked to write a story is different than the sort of work they produce when asked to write a teaching text. By seeing what individual students can do in relation to the descriptors for kindergarten, you'll begin to see some of the specific ways you can support children's growth.

GETTING READY

Since this is your first unit of the year, it will be important to organize materials so that you can launch your writing workshop well. *A Guide to the Writing Workshop* will help you do this, but for now, we want to mention that you'll want to make sure you have paper in a writing center that students can use. Most of you will start off by giving children a choice between blank paper and paper with a large picture space with one line. Based on the results of your assessments, some of you may include the option of paper with a line or two. The unit will bring your students toward writing books, so there will come a time, later in the unit, beyond which you will probably not have single sheets available. At the start of the unit, however, it would be best not to provide the option of writing in booklets. Let that come as a surprise a few days into

the workshop. Once you do provide booklets, keep in mind that the booklets can have more or fewer lines depending on the amount of writing children are actually doing underneath the labeled pictures.

You will want to provide your students with writing caddies that hold the tools that need to be available on the tables—tools such as pens, a date stamp, a mini-stapler, tape, extra paper, Post-its, and strips and flaps that students can add on to their writing. You will also want to have a pocket folder for each student.

You, too, will need some materials. You will not only want to create your own pieces of writing, but you will want to have some chart paper on which you and your students can write some class pieces together. You will want to have collected a few mentor texts that you can use to show your students how published writers, in your library, create teaching books and stories. We use Donald Crews's *Freight Train* and Phyllis Root's *Creak! Said the Bed,* and if you've purchased the trade book pack of children's literature that is available with this grade, you have those there. You will be creating, with your students, a couple of charts to support them in learning, first, what they can do when they are done and, second, what makes for a good story. You will also be using a checklist with your students that you will want to have ready; you will find each unit's checklist in the online resources.

What you need most are some colleagues who will be teaching alongside you and will join you in learning from what your children do.

ONLINE DIGITAL RESOURCES

A variety of resources to accompany this and the other Grade K Units of Study in Opinion, Information, and Narrative Writing are available in the online resources. To access and download all the digital resources for this grade-level set:

1. Go to **www.heinemann.com** and click the link in the upper right to log in. (If you do not have an account yet, you will need to create one.)

2. **Enter the following registration code** in the box to register your product: **WUOS_GK**

3. Enter the security information requested, obtained from within your unit book.

4. Once you have registered your product it will appear in the list of "View my registered Online Resources, Videos, and eBooks." (Note: You only need register once; then each time you return to your account, just click the "My Online Resources" link to access these materials.)

(You may keep copies of these resources on up to six of your own computers or devices. By downloading the files you acknowledge that they are for your individual or classroom use and that neither the resources nor the product code will be distributed or shared.)

We Are All Writers

Putting Ideas on Paper with Pictures and Words

IN THIS SESSION, you'll teach students that young writers think of something that they know about and use pictures and words to put their ideas on paper.

GETTING READY

✔ Desks clustered to support the conversations

✔ Plans for your own short piece of writing, both important to you and true (see Teaching)

✔ Chart paper and markers

✔ Two mentor texts you'll hold up to show the class. You'll use one as a model throughout the first part of the unit and the second for the second half of the unit. *Freight Train*, by Donald Crews (1992) and *Creak! Said the Bed*, by Phyllis Root (2010) are used here (see Connection).

✔ Paper for each child—blank pages and pages with a large box drawn on each and a few write-on lines below the box

✔ Pens and markers for each table of writers, for after the minilesson

✔ A way to take notes on your conferences. A notebook with a page for each child, in alphabetical order, might be helpful.

TO LAUNCH YOUR WRITING WORKSHOP, gather your youngsters close and tell them one of the great secrets of literacy. "All the books on our shelves that bring us such wonderful stories and ideas, were written by people like you and me. We, too, can put stories and knowledge on the page. This very day, each of you will be an author.

"Let me show you how to write a book," you'll say, and quickly demonstrate the gist of the writing process. Then you'll send your children off to draw and to write, putting something they know and care about onto the page.

I imagine you thinking, "Really? Maybe you don't know my kids—but mine come to me not knowing the alphabet, let alone having the skills to write on their own."

But I do know your youngsters, and this writing workshop is designed for them, precisely. Even though some children will make drawings that are nonrepresentative, not even attempting letter-like forms, one of the most powerful things you can possibly do is to invite youngsters to step into the role of being avid writers. Your children will approximate—they will pretend—but that is how young people learn many things. The wise parent will say to a toddler, "Could you help me sweep up this dirt?" And then, when the toddler scrubs back and forth with the broom, the parent will say, "Thanks for your help!" In this session, you will be educating in a very similar fashion. The power of the session will depend on your confidence that every one of your children can think of a topic she knows a lot about and then put that knowledge onto the page, drawing and writing as best she can.

If you are uneasy about this, remember that during dress up, children role-play their way into being kings and queens, waitresses and astronauts, and you probably don't worry that somehow you are letting them flounder in roles that are beyond them. In the same way, then, enjoy their approximations and role playing as writers, and trust that we'll help you teach into that work as quickly as possible. Your teaching will accomplish something important if children believe that they belong to the world of written language.

You also will give yourself a chance to see how much they can do on Day One.

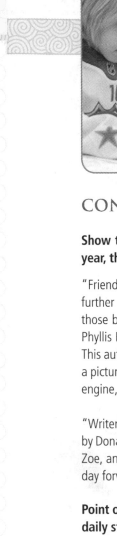

We Are All Writers

Putting Ideas on Paper with Pictures and Words

CONNECTION

Show the children different kinds of books, pointing out that writers wrote them all. Tell children that this year, they'll write too, producing books like those circling the meeting area.

"Friends, scoot up close because I have something important to tell you." I gave the children thirty seconds to move further up on the rug, and then I leaned in and continued. "We're sitting here because—look all around you! See all those books? Each one was written by a different writer." I held up *Creak! Said the Bed* and said, "A writer named Phyllis Root wrote this. See? Here's her name on the front cover." I pointed to it. "And look at this one! *Freight Train*! This author, Donald Crews, wrote a *teaching book* that teaches us all about the different parts of a train. Each page has a picture of a different part of the train, like the different freight cars. One page has the front of the train, like the steam engine, and another has the caboose. Each page has a label next to the part of the train to name it.

"Writers write to make stuff—stories," I held up *Creak! Said the Bed*, "and teaching books, too." I held up *Freight Train* by Donald Crews. "And this year, *you* are going to write books as well. That means *you*, Annie, and *you*, Owen, and *you*, Zoe, and *you*, Margay, and all of you." I swept my arm across the room, indicating each and every child. "So from this day forward, I'm going to call you *writers*."

Point out that if you are going to call children *writers*, they need time to write, and use that to introduce the daily structure of a writing workshop.

"Of course, if I'm going to call you *writers*, you'll need time to actually write, to make stuff—stories and teaching books, too. So every day we'll have what writers all around the world call a *writing workshop*. We'll gather in this spot to learn what writers do. We'll sit, surrounded by books, and soon, we'll add *your* books to these shelves."

❖ **Name the teaching point.**

"So, writers, today, what I want to teach you is that it is not just grown-ups like Donald Crews who write to teach people what they know. You can do that as well. You think of something you know about, and then with drawings and writing, you put what you know on the paper."

We are on the first day of school and already you are offering children the excitement of a lifetime of writing, of bookmaking! Make sure you let your excitement show. Give children something to be wide-eyed about and proud of on their very first day!

Your confidence and enthusiasm will carry most children along. No matter how tentative and insecure you may feel, role-play your way into being confident about yourself and your children because they will hitch a ride on your enthusiasm. It's scary to begin, but every day teachers bravely send children off to draw and write, and lo and behold, the miracle happens. Children draw squiggles and turtles and tall buildings, they make writing-like graphics or alphabet letters that float across the page, and some record long stories. No matter what they do, children put themselves onto the page.

TEACHING

Demonstrate how you go about making a teaching text—coming up with topics, then picturing those topics, and then getting ready to put what you know on the page.

"Let's each do some writing to teach people what we know about. Watch me and then you can do it as well. We first need to think, 'What do I know about that I could teach other people?' Hmm, . . . Are you thinking, 'What do *I* know about?'" After pausing for everyone to begin thinking, I began listing possible topics. "I could write about TV shows or dogs or bikes. I have a bike so I could teach other people about bikes. Or I could write to teach people about gardens, because my Grandma has one. That's it! I'll write about gardens.

"Now I am going to put what I know on the page by drawing and writing. First, let me remember how my grandma's garden looks." I looked up toward the ceiling, conjuring up the image, then I started to draw, saying, "This is a tomato plant, held up by a stick, and there are three of these in my Grandma's garden. I'll add the little thing that ties the plant to the stick." I quickly added the words, 'Grandma's garden' under the picture, not discussing why or how I did that.

ACTIVE ENGAGEMENT

Channel writers to think of a topic they could teach others and to tell what they might put on their page.

"Right now, think of what you know about that you could teach others. Picture it." Silently, I pictured my topic again, modeling and giving children time to do this, too. Then, a few seconds later, "Tell the people near you what *you* will draw and write about in your teaching piece."

I crouched alongside Liam, who quickly blurted, "I am thinking I could write about cats because I have one and she is black, and really, really, really cute. She eats cat food." Then he poked Margay in the shoulder and said, "You go."

Before children finished talking, I interrupted. "Writers, after you picture your topic, you need to put it on the paper. You can draw it and write words, just like Donald Crews does." I showed a page of one of his nonfiction books.

LINK

Remind children that they can write to teach people things, just like grown-ups.

"It is not just *grown-ups* who can write to teach people things. You can each write about something you know, teaching others about that topic." Then I said, "If you know what you will put on your paper, thumbs up. When I see that you are ready, I will give you paper and a pen so that you can get started." Hands shot up, and I provisioned and dispersed half the class. Once they were settled, I did the same for the other half.

In the center of the tables you will want to have more paper that students can use to draw and write. There should be space for them to write their name at the top and a big box for them to draw in as well as a line (or two) below the picture box. This is helpful to have, especially for students who are already able to write with letters and sounds. These students should be encouraged from the start to not only label but to also write sentences below their drawings. If you have students who write with random strings of letters on the line below, do not be alarmed. They are approximating what they know about writing and how books go. But you will want to encourage these writers to label and put letters and sounds next to the pictures so that you can help them develop phonemic awareness.

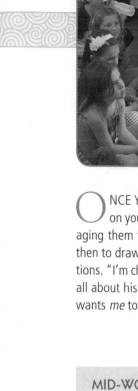

Anticipating the Challenges of These First Days

ONCE YOUR CHILDREN have dispersed to their workplaces, you will need to "put on your roller skates" and start moving quickly among your youngsters, encouraging them to think of something they know, to envision that thing, that topic, and then to draw and perhaps write about it. As you do this, you will have a million questions. "I'm channeling them to write a teaching piece, but what if a child wants to write all about his mother? That's not exactly nonfiction. Do I support that? What if a child wants *me* to draw for him? Do I agree to do that?"

You will be able to make wise decisions as long as you keep in the front of your mind the fact that for today, your goals are for children to feel as if they are insiders in the world of written language, for them to carry on as writers with as much independence as possible, and for them to begin to grasp the big ideas of the discipline of writing. One big idea is this: a writer has a meaning to convey and works to put that meaning onto the page so that the page can be passed to someone else, and that person can see what the writer has done and make meaning from it. Another big idea is that

MID-WORKSHOP TEACHING   Writers Work on Their Writing

"Writers," I said loudly, and did a 360-degree scan of the room. "I need your full attention, so pens down, please. Eyes up here, please." I did another 360-degree scan, and when I had children's attention, I continued. "Earlier, I said that you would all be writers today, just like Donald Crews and Phyllis Root." I held up their books. "And watching you, some of you *have* been working just like real writers." Turning to one child, I continued. "Clarissa, will you get back to work so the rest of us can watch you being a writer and say what we see?" Clarissa, sitting smack in the middle of the room, giggled a little and returned to work.

"Do you see that Clarissa is holding a marker in her hand and writing *on the paper*, just like real authors do! Is she writing on her arm?"

The children chorused, "Nooooooo."

Then I posed a sequence of other questions: "Is she tapping her marker on the table like this? Is she twirling around in her chair so much that she doesn't get any work done?" Each question was met with a chorus of "Nooooos."

"Right now, I'm going to take a picture of Clarissa, working like a writer, and we can put that picture up on our chart so we can all remember that this is what it looks like to be a writer." I clicked a picture with my cell phone. "I bet that pretty soon I'll have pictures of every one of you looking like real writers!

"*And* there is another way I can tell that Clarissa is a writer. I can look at her work." I held up her page of drawings and walked the page solemnly around the room so children, dispersed at desks and tables, could get a glance. "Clarissa has drawn a whole lot about dance class. Remember how I put the tomatoes into my writing about the garden? Well, Clarissa has put special dance shoes, and a dance leotard, and a dance bar, and all kinds of stuff onto her paper. I bet she is even going to write some letters beside her pictures!

"Tell someone near you what you are going to put into your writing." I let the children talk. After a minute of moving among children, giving them a thumbs-up sign, I voiced over quietly. "I know you are dying to work on your writing. Get going!"

(continues)

As Students Continue Working . . .

"How terrific. Deja is writing all about the school bus! Jose is writing about hamsters. Great topics!"

"When you picture your subject," I called out, "remember to add in little tiny details, like the string holding my tomato plants onto their sticks."

"Once you've drawn something, you can write words beside your picture. Like I am going to write *tomato* beside my plant so people will know." Then I muttered, as if to myself, "Tomatoes! *tttttt* like Tom! *T!* *T* for *tomatoes.*" I then said the word again and soon had added an *M.* "It'd be terrific to see some of you adding words beside your pictures, too."

writers look at the books that others have written and think, "I could do something like that too!" Keeping these goals in mind, you will probably be very accepting of children's efforts. If a five-year-old decides that what he knows most about is his mom, by all means, you'll encourage that youngster to use writing to teach the world all about his mom. If a child wants *you* to draw or write for her, resist the urge to lend a hand, as this may create dependency. With all the lightness and confidence in the world, you'll seize that request as an invitation to support approximation. "Oh my goodness, you wouldn't want *my* writing on your paper. What have you drawn? Oh! Cool! So just write that right here. Just write it any ol' way, as best you can." Then if the child writes something that looks like chicken scratch, say, "Good job! Where else do you want to put some writing?"

If you are worried that your children may not be able to sustain work for an entire writing workshop, you are wise. After twenty minutes, the room may begin to unravel. You'll rely on mid-workshop teaching points as a support structure for keeping writers working; early in the year, these interludes function as stones across the river, helping the students last through the entire workshop. It is not uncommon to have several mid-workshop teaching points in a day's writing workshop, especially during these first days. It is also entirely possible that the writing workshop will be abbreviated for this first week. Because you have not yet had a chance to teach writers to carry on with any independence, to go from one piece of writing to another, to add details to their drawings, to spell as best they can, or any of those other lessons, your children will very likely not yet know how to sustain themselves, and so you'll stop while the going is good, shifting to a share meeting once many children seem to be at loose ends.

You will probably find that you need to be physically present in all corners of the room, making it impossible to interact one-on-one very much. Instead, you'll pull up a chair alongside a table full of writers, asking all the children to stop what they are doing and to talk with you. Then you might, for example, name what one child has done that seems to you to be exactly right. Alternatively, you could name what the entire table full of children seem to be doing that you hope they continue to do. "I love the way the group of you has gotten started. You didn't wait for me to come around and help each one of you, one by one. No! Instead you've done exactly what real writers do. You've picked up your pens and gotten started putting what you know onto the page. And you are adding details, too. That is so, so smart. Get back to work, and I am just going to admire what you do for a minute." In a similar fashion, you could extol the way some writers have remembered to record their names or the way they have been brave enough to try spelling something they don't really know how to spell or have helped each other or drawn in ways that show action. We refer to those interactions as *table compliments*, and they have amazing power.

Becoming a Club of Writers

Ask different children to share their work by holding it high for the world to see.

I convened the children in the meeting area, and after they were settled, said, "Writers, there's a lot of great writing in this room! How many of you put something on the page? Great! When I point to you, hold your writing up high so we can all admire it." I acted like a conductor, with children proudly hoisting pictures and writing overhead.

Point out that writers work with support from each other, and suggest the class become a giant writing club (with a club name and all).

"Your writing has been teaching me about so many things. That got me thinking about something else I want to tell you. Writers don't work alone. No way! Writers find people who will listen to their writing and who will say, 'I like this part,' or 'You should add such and such.' *And* writers get ideas from looking at what other writers do.

"I was thinking that all of us—in this class—could become kind of like a writing club for each other, and we could help each other write like real authors. Do you like the idea of us becoming a writing club? Thumbs up."

When children signaled with thumbs up, I said, "You definitely need a name for a club, right? Who has an idea for what we could name our writing club?" Hands shot up. "Turn and tell people sitting near you a good name for our writing club."

As children talked, I crouched among them, gathering a list of possibilities. "Here are some of the names I heard you suggest," I said, and in a jiffy, the class had decided on the name Super Writers.

Now that the class is a club of writers, rally children to learn from what several writers did.

"So, Super Writers, if we are a club of writers, we need to share our writing, right? Let's all look at Fabian's writing (see Figure 1–1) because it can teach us about baseball. Do you see his drawings here? And look what else he added—words! He labeled his drawings with letters! I bet you know what this is, right? Look, here is the letter *B* for /b/ *ball*! Can you tell where Fabian labeled himself? He wrote, 'me.' That's right, look, here is the *M* for *me*! Right next to the picture of himself playing baseball.

FIG. 1–1 Fabian's writing: *Bat. This is a baseball. I know how to play. This is me with curly hair.* (Labels: *Me. Baseball.*)

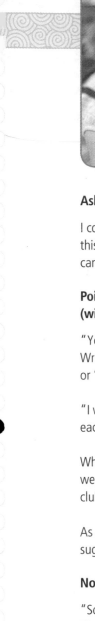

"Is any writer in this club of ours getting an idea for something *you* can do when you get more time for writing tomorrow? Thumbs up if Fabian's writing is giving you ideas for what you can do." The children signaled "yes."

"Let's look at one more! Here is Joseline's piece! (See Figure 1–2.) Let's read it together. I am going to move my finger and touch each thing in Joseline's piece about her bedroom. Here is Joseline's bed. Let me see what else there is. Oh, here is Joseline's dresser! And what else do we see? Oh yeah! Here is Joseline's desk!"

Joseline piped in, "And my dirty clothes on the floor!" And I agreed that I'd missed that.

"Do you see how Joseline has included *so much* about her bedroom? You can do that in your writing, too! You can try to fill up the pages with information just like Joseline did!

"Will those of you wearing red stand up?" They did, and I noted they were fairly well distributed among the group. "Share your writing with others who are near you, and touch each thing that you drew and say what it is, and then read what you wrote. I am sure the rest of you too will see things in your friends' writing that you could try in your writing tomorrow!"

After a minute or two, I said, "Writers, we need to stop now, but the good news is that you will be writing again tomorrow!"

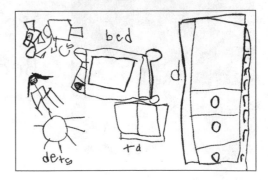

FIG. 1–2   Joseline's writing: *This is my room. I have my bed. This is the blanket. I have my animals at the end of the bed. I have a table next to my bed. This is the dresser where I put my clothes. This is my desk. I am sitting at the desk.* (Labels: *Bed. Dresser. Desk. Table. Clothes.*)

FIG. 1–3   Another example, Isabella's writing, "Animals Have Names." *Pony, Elephant, Pony, Horse, Horse.*

Writers Know that "When We Are Done, We Have Just Begun."

WHAT A TREASURE TROVE OF INFORMATION these early pieces provide! Study them well and record your findings.

The examples of students' work from the previous session will fill you with resolve to teach a thousand things, but frankly, you won't be able to teach anyone much of anything until your children can sustain themselves enough that you are freed from simply managing and are able to teach. This means, for starters, that you will need to teach children how they can sustain their own work. This will be an especially important lesson because chances are good that not many of your children will begin the year with much staying power. You will know that is the case for your students if, during your first day's writing workshop, you experienced the phenomenon of children starting and finishing their work within about ten minutes and then popping up to say, "I'm done!" You will want to teach children the saying, "When you are done, you have just begun."

Although there are management reasons to teach children to keep going beyond their first draft—and if children can't sustain themselves, you won't be able to interact with individuals and small groups long enough to demonstrate and coach them—the message that writers don't just dash something onto the page and then declare it a day also addresses something at the very core of writing. The writing workshop approach to teaching writing is founded on the principle that even young children can write in ways that are not all that different from the ways that professional writers write. Just as five-year-olds who are studying floating and sinking in science can experience a simplified version of the scientific method, your children will be experiencing a simplified version of the writing process. Even though your children are just four or five years old, they can approximate the process of writing that is integral to the work of professional writers. And for professional writers, nothing is more essential than the rhythm of pulling in to write, then pulling back to reread, to assess, and to think, "Have I really said what I want to say?"

In this session you teach students that writers reread and add onto their first draft, adding more detail and information through pictures and words. And then, yes, writers do move on to more writing.

IN THIS SESSION, you'll teach students that writers look back at their writing and see if they can add more to it.

GETTING READY

✔ Student writing from Session 1 (see Teaching, Active Engagement, and Link)

✔ Your own writing from Session 1 (see Teaching)

✔ Chart paper and markers

✔ "When We Are Done, We Have Just Begun" chart (see Share)

Writers Know that "When We Are Done, We Have Just Begun."

CONNECTION

Remind children that today and every day, the writing workshop will begin with a minilesson. Remind them of what happens in a minilesson to induct them into their role.

"Good morning, Super Writers! When you come to our meeting area this morning, please bring with you the piece you wrote yesterday. And sit on that writing, so you will have it close by if you need it."

After children convened and scrunched up close to where I sat, I began. "Writers, I'm glad to see you sitting on your bottoms, pulled close. Thank you. Today and every day, we'll start the writing workshop with a minilesson. In a minilesson, I will always teach you—I will show you—something that writers do often, something you can do as well. During the first part of the minilesson, your job is to listen and to learn. You don't talk much during that part. Then after I teach you something, you can all try it on the rug. After that, I'll send you off to work on your writing, and I'll remind you that when you write, you might try what you learned today or on earlier days."

Suggest children recruit family members to write as well. Use that prospect as an opportunity to get them recalling and teaching a pretend grandmother how to write a teaching piece.

"How many of you told your mom or your grandmother or your friend or someone else that you are a writer now?" Children signaled with thumbs up or down. "You might even get those people to be writers too, if you have paper at home. Then you could have a writing club at school *and* at home!

"Let's pretend I am your grandma. Here, I'll dress up as Grandma." I put glasses on the tip of my nose and wrapped my sweater around me like a shawl. Then, folding my hands like a well-meaning elderly woman, I said, "Good morning. What's this I hear about being writers? How can I be a writer?"

The kids giggled.

Shifting out of the grandma role, I spoke with urgency to the children, "Quick! Help each other think what you can tell Grandma about what writers do. Turn and talk!"

At the start of the year, you'll weave into your teaching bits of instruction on how writing workshops go, naming both your role and children's roles. As the year progresses, you may need to tuck in little reminders of these norms.

I was trying to have some fun with this minilesson—adding in a little playacting. If this is not you, then by all means find a different way to bring some spirit into the minilesson! Encourage joyfulness and the essence of play, and you also encourage writers.

As the children turned to talk with each other, I moved among them, helping them recall the previous day's learning—coaching them to say something to the effect of writers think of things that they know and then draw and write about those things, adding in detailed information.

Returning to my chair at the front of the meeting area, I said, "Eyes up here," and waited. Then I stepped back into the role of Grandma and said, "So, can you tell me what writers do?"

Kevin started. "First you have to think."

"Yes, Kevin. I have to think . . . hmm . . . of . . . ?"

"Then you have to think really, really hard. Then you make it." Emma said.

"I have to think of a topic and really, really picture it in my head and then I just make it on the paper—drawing all the details I can. Is that it?" Shifting out of the Grandma role, I said, "Writers, now I am going to teach you one more thing you can do as writers—and one more thing you can teach anyone you know who might want to be in a writing club with you."

❖ **Name the teaching point.**

"Today I want to teach you that *after* writers write what they know about a topic, they don't just say, 'I'm done' and relax. No way! Instead, writers say, 'I'm going to look back on my writing and see if I can *add more* to it.' Writers revise."

TEACHING

Set children up to encourage you to look back on yesterday's writing, seeing if you can add more.

"You and I both made teaching pieces yesterday. Get yours out, and I'll get mine out as well." Soon we were all holding our writing. "I have a lot of stuff already in my garden book: tomatoes, a rake. So, writers, do you think after we have put some stuff we know onto the page, we can just say, 'I'm done?'" To illustrate that alternative, I pretended to fall asleep, nestled against my hand.

"No!" the children called. "You gotta add more."

"You are right. Writers have a saying: 'When you are done, you have just begun.' Now that we are done writing our pieces, we can look back on what we have written, read what is on our page, and think, 'What *else* do I know that I could add?'"

Ask children to watch what you do as a writer, and then act out the wrong way to do things— shoving scrunched-up paper into a folder, leaving open markers in the can, hoarding five markers. Then invite children to critique your behaviors. They'll laugh, but they'll also learn.

Demonstrate "rereading" each item in your drawing, pointing as you name the item, and then generating more content to add.

"Watch me do that with my writing, and then you will have a chance to do it with yours."

I looked at my writing and then very deliberately took out my finger and pointed under each item on my page, saying a sentence or two about each, making my oral text feel like an all-about information book. "This is a tomato plant. It is held onto a stick with string so it doesn't fall over."

Then I shifted. "This is a rake. I wonder what I should do now. I could start a new piece of writing about something new." I gestured toward taking up another sheet of paper. "But wait! I notice I have more space on my paper. Hmm, . . . What can I add? I do know more about gardens. I know! This doesn't tell about the *bugs*! I'm going to add the bugs. Worms, too." And I started to draw, then interrupted myself to teach.

Debrief, emphasizing that as a writer, you need to decide whether to add onto a piece you've already begun writing or to start a new one.

"Writers, did you see that I reread my writing, putting my finger under each thing on my paper, and then I thought, 'What *else* can I add?' Writers don't just work on a piece and then say, 'I'm done.' Writers have a saying: 'When you are done, you have just begun.'"

ACTIVE ENGAGEMENT

Recruit one writer to function as a case in point, and rally the class to help that one writer think about things he could add to his teaching piece.

"Derrick, will you come up here?" Derrick threaded his way to the front of the meeting. "Writers, Derrick has a lot of stuff already on the page about our classroom! Let's pretend he said, 'I'm done.'" And then, pretending to be Derrick, I feigned falling asleep. "What would you tell Derrick?"

The children chimed in that Derrick needed to do more, to reread, to add on. I agreed. "You all know that writers don't just do a little writing and then say, 'I'm done!' Young writers reread what they have written, touching each thing they have put onto the page and saying what they've got on the paper.

"So, Derrick, are you ready to do what writers do?" I asked. And Derrick reread his page, touching the depiction of the classroom and saying aloud, "The kids, the teacher, the flag, and the pencil sharpener."

I pressed Derrick to tell us what he needed to do next. Derrick answered, "Ask what *else* should I put?" Nodding, I said, "So, Derrick, what else might you put into your writing to teach people about our classroom?" As Derrick scrunched up his face to consider this, I said to the rest of the class, "Turn and tell the person beside you other things that Derrick could put into his teaching page."

At this early juncture, what you are instilling in children is a sense of the writer's process. Even when children are just making scribbles on one sheet of paper and declaring that a finished piece, you can teach revision. Show the writer that he or she can look back and think, "What else can I say?" and then add more onto the page! That's revision. Adding more. Of course, for many children, this will be adding details to the drawing—seagulls over the beach and shells dotting the shore. For kindergartners, revision first involves adding details into drawings or drawing a second picture, and only later involves adding more words.

I listened in as Owen said, "Uhhh, he could add the hamster cage?" And Zoe, rising up on her knees, added, "Yeah, and the dress up stuff!" Soon several children had shared their ideas with the whole class.

Debrief in a way that highlights the transferable lessons you hope writers have learned.

"How do those suggestions sound, Derrick?" I asked, and in response, Derrick tucked his head down, and started working zealously to add the requisite items to his page.

"Writers, look what Derrick is doing now! He is revising. All the authors of all these beautiful books on our shelves did the very same work that Derrick has just done. They worked hard to put what they know on the page, and then when they were done, they didn't just say, 'I'm done' (and go to sleep). No way! When they were done, they went back to work. They reread what they had written and thought, 'What *else* do I know that I could teach people?' and then they added on."

LINK

Channel children to decide whether to add onto their teaching piece or to start another.

"Earlier, I asked you to bring the page you were working on yesterday to our meeting today. Right now, will each of you try rereading your own page of writing, as you saw Derrick do? And as you reread, squeeze your mind to think, 'Is there more I could add?' Remember, writers, *you* are in charge of your writing. *You* need to make a decision about whether your teaching piece needs more or whether it is time for you to move on to another piece." Kindergartners don't read silently, so the room was filled with quiet voices. Then, I said, "Tell the people sitting near you what you might add, and show them where you will put the new information." I listened, and as I identified writers who seemed raring to get started, I sent them to their writing spots.

When you say, "Off you go" at the end of the minilesson, get the class to join you in watching a group of children do whatever it is you hope all children will do. Say, "Let's watch as they go quickly to their seats, get their supplies, and get to work." While children do this, name what you notice they're doing to the rest of the class, who'll still be at your feet. "Watch how the red table is walking straight to their writing nooks, not talking as they go! See how each person got out his or her writing," and so on. "Which table of writers feels ready to do just as good a job as the red table? Okay blue table, let's see how you get started writing."

Helping Students Get Ideas onto Paper

AS SOON AS YOU HAVE DISPERSED STUDENTS, you'll immediately want to begin moving around the room, helping settle students into their writing. Try doing this first by relying especially on gestures, as you will find that they are incredibly helpful, and they allow you to be present in all corners of the room within a minute or two. So tap on one child's paper; put another child's page in front of her; put a pen in a third child's hand. Give a child a decisive thumbs up. Make a "What's going on?" gesture to another.

After two or three minutes of this sort of settling work, you will probably want to do voiceovers. When you do these voiceovers, you are not asking every child to stop, freeze, and look at you. Instead, you are talking like a sportscaster above the hubbub.

If you find a line of students forming behind you, send those students off to continue working. "Wait! Writers need to keep working," you can say to the line. "Writers need to be in their seats, adding more work to the page. I'll be coming to each of your tables to admire your work."

There will be a few kids who are acting out, drawing on their arms, making towers with their markers. Try a positive approach. First, notice what others are doing well and lavish praise on them. Usually the result is as predictable as clockwork. The one child whose behavior was problematic begins to do whatever has earned your attention and praise.

Because your presence will be felt everywhere, children are apt to settle down fairly quickly to their writing, and once they are settled, you will be able to conduct a conference or two. If you have access to the DVD *Big Lessons from Small Writers* (Heinemann, 2005), see Amanda's conference with Harold, my all-time favorite video of a teacher conferring with a kindergarten child. In that conference, Harold doesn't know what to write about (he's actually writing Small Moment stories, not teaching pages), and Amanda tells him that when she is stuck, she thinks about things that she does. Then she demonstrates, and does so by generating a little list of things that she knows

Harold does. "I could write about when I ride my bike, 'cause I do that a lot," Amanda says. "I could write about. . . ." Sometimes it helps to make the sources of your list really explicit, like suggesting you'll think about things you do and know about at home and things you do and know about in school. "At home, I know a lot about TV. I know about cooking. Here in the classroom I know a lot about books. What else is in this classroom that I know a lot about? Oh, yeah! I know a lot about blocks." Notice,

---

MID-WORKSHOP TEACHING
Writers Write More Than One Piece in a Day

"Eyes on me, writers. I love all the ways you are finding to add on to your books. All these cool little details are teaching me even more about the things you know well.

"When I was sitting at the blue table today, out of the corner of my eye, I saw Yatri do something very important. She finished working on her paper, and I wondered what she was going to do, so I watched. And then, do you know what I saw? I saw her reach over to the paper tray, and get *another piece of paper*! Yatri had finished her first piece, but she didn't say, 'I'm done now' and plop her head down on the table to take a little snooze. She did what writers do, which is to start another piece of writing! Bravo, Yatri! I bet we could all do that. I've only known you for a short while, but I already can tell that you all have so many ideas to share. Five years worth of ideas! So I want to remind you that writers don't wait for a teacher to tell them that it is okay to start another piece of writing. No way! As soon as a writer has done all he or she can do to *one* piece of writing, that writer gets more paper and starts another piece of writing! Look at the paper tray in the middle of your table. I can almost hear that paper calling out, 'Use me! Use me!'"

"I see Zoe. She has already started to fill up her page with drawings and writing."

"Owen is not just making one thing on the page; he is starting to draw something else about his topic."

"Wow, Sebastian, I just watched how you listened for the click when you put the cap back onto the marker! What a great way to take care of your tools!"

"Remember, when you are done, you've just begun! Read what you wrote! Ask, 'What can I add?'"

"Wow, Casey was about to say she couldn't read what she wrote, but then she remembered she could point to her picture and read that!"

in this instance, that the teacher helps the writer generate a small collection of topics, giving the writer additional practice at this, as well as a bank to draw upon.

It is sometimes hard to discern the intended meaning in a child's work. Sometimes children's drawings will not be very representational, and they'll forget what they intended to make. Daniel's piece (see Figure 2–1) may or may not be a representational drawing of something he knows about. Only through a conversation with the writer will you be

able to know for sure. In these situations, it is important for you to show the child that readers work hard to figure out what a text says. "That looks like a building. Could it have been the school? Is that your grandpa's house?" Sometimes the writer's face will light up. "Yes, yes, that's it!" You can help the writer add more detail so that another time, it is easier to remember. You may want to scrawl a little cursive note to yourself, off in some corner of the text, cuing yourself in to what the writer told you so that another day, this cheat sheet can help you support the child's efforts to "read" the writing.

Of course, some children will draw what they know how to draw rather than topics on which they have expertise. You may find yourself noticing that a child has drawn a bird and a heart, presumably because this is his drawing repertoire. "Oh my goodness. What are you teaching us about birds? That is so cool that you know a lot about birds." If the child's picture consists of rainbows and shamrocks, you may need to be a bit more clear. Sophie has drawn some things that delight her (see Figure 2–2), and frankly there's nothing wrong with a little delight! It's also important for her to learn that her ideas and experiences are worth putting on the page, to communicate with others.

Although much of your teaching will support children as they learn to decide on a meaning and then to use whatever they have at their disposal to encode that meaning onto the page, you will absolutely want to also support children's oral language. If a child tells you his drawing is a plane, try to use active listening and responsiveness to help the child generate a lot of language about that plane. Say back, "Ah, so it is a plane!" And then wait. Say prompts such as, "Tell me more about this plane." When the child tells you, "It goes fast," say that back, and be impressed.

FIG. 2–1 Daniel's shapes may represent figures and objects in a place, or they may not. It's important to talk to the writer about his intentions.

FIG. 2–2 Sophie's drawing seems to be a way of decorating her paper, rather than an effort to communicate her knowledge about a topic.

Learning Systems and Tools for the Writing Workshop
Table Monitors and Anchor Charts

Roll out the system of table monitors.

Once most children were done, I said, "Six of you—one person at each table—have agreed to be our first table monitors. Will you six stand up?" They did. "Table monitors, show us how you can carefully collect your table's tools and writing, returning them to our writing center. Everyone will have a chance to do this important job, so let's watch how they do it." I gave the children a couple of minutes to complete this task. "Wow! Thanks for taking such great care of our writing tools and supplies!"

Introduce the "When We Are Done, We Have Just Begun" chart.

"Nice job, everyone! From this day forward, then, and for the rest of your life, remember the ways writers can work. We saw Clarissa working yesterday, didn't we?" I said, holding up a photo of her hard at work. "We saw Yatri working today when she reached for more paper and started a new piece, and I saw lots of you adding onto your writing. I started to make a chart of the ways writers work. Up here it says, 'When we are done, we've just begun.' Down here I wrote and drew the three things I saw people doing today. Can you tell what they are? I'll read them to you. 'We can add to our pictures. We can add to our words. We can start a new piece.' From now on, when you are about to say, 'I'm done!' you can look at this chart instead. Pretty impressive!"

When We Are Done, We Have Just Begun

We can:

- add to our pictures
- add to our words
- start a new piece

Carrying on Independently as Writers

IT IS HARD TO OVEREMPHASIZE the importance of establishing clear structures and routines so children can carry on with independence during writing time. You need to imagine kids starting, working on, and completing their writing as best they are able, moving from one text to another with verve and confidence, even though the work they produce will probably not dazzle you at this early point in the year. Chances are good that many of your children's "finished pieces" will consist of an underdeveloped scrawl and little more. And, that's okay—for now.

For children to carry on with independence, you'll want to think about the routines that you need to teach explicitly. Certainly, kids will need to learn the expectations you have of them, such as when to give you their attention (many teachers use a catchy refrain like "One, two, three, all eyes on me!") and how to move around the room quickly and quietly. Children will need to know how to find any supplies they'll need—pens, pencils, different kinds of paper, the date stamp—so that they can easily and seamlessly keep themselves going during writing workshop. Most of all, they need to know what's expected of them during different parts of the workshop. You will want to teach children to move to and from the meeting area quickly and sit on their bottoms, hands to themselves, on assigned rug spots. Then, too, you will need to teach children what they are expected to do when, in the middle of a minilesson, you say, "Turn and talk" and then, a minute or two later, "Eyes back here."

You will no doubt come up with other systems for kids to carry on with independence, and you may even recruit your kids to think of their own ways to keep themselves going. It's never too early to convey to kids that they are their own best resource during a workshop. One way or another, students need to know where to find the day's schedule, the supplies they need, and their spot at the table and on the rug. As they gain independence, encourage children to be problem solvers. When a child acts with notable self-reliance, you may want to celebrate this: "Writers, will you look here for a minute? I want to tell you about

IN THIS SESSION, you'll teach students that writers come up with solutions to their problems and carry on writing.

GETTING READY

✔ Your own writing from Session 2 (see Teaching)

✔ Paper, to start a new piece of your own writing (see Teaching)

✔ Date stamps (see Share)

✔ Two-pocket folders for each student, with a red dot sticker on one pocket and a green dot sticker on the other pocket (see Share)

✔ "When We Are Done, We Have Just Begun" chart from Session 2

the smart work Pedro did. Pedro finished his writing. But do you think he just sat there and said, 'Oh, no, what will I do now? Oh, no, oh, no.' No way! Pedro solved his own problem. And you know what he did?"

"It's never too early to convey to kids that they are their own best resource during a workshop."

When children are able to carry on with independence, writing as best they can, you will be able to move among them, teaching into their work. That is, you are only free to teach if kids are not relying on you for every little thing. Only then can you pull a group of children in to huddle and show them how to write *lion*, stretching the first sound out, /lllll/, and then thinking what letter makes that sound—*l*!—and popping that letter onto the page. That instruction will be important, and it will be important, too, to show children that writers reread their writing by putting a finger under each object they've drawn, saying aloud what that object is, and then asking themselves, "Did I put everything here that needs to go? Did I leave off my dog's tail? Oh no!" But you can't do that teaching until you explicitly teach your children to be resourceful, brave, independent writers. This means that your first goal—helping writers work with confidence and independence, at whatever level of work they can pull off—actually enables the next goal, which is for you to teach in ways that dramatically lift the level of what kids can do. Today will go a long way toward accomplishing that instruction.

Carrying on Independ

What they will need: nothing

CONNECTION

Playact that you are stuck and dependent, bothering everyone with requests for direction, setting the stage for you to emphasize the need for resourcefulness.

Once children were convened on the rug, I slouched in my chair and let out a big sigh. "I don't know what to do today. I already wrote my garden page, and I don't know what to add. No one told me what to do." I sighed dramatically again and made a desperate face.

Then I tapped one child, sitting nearby, on the shoulder and whined, "Yatri, what do I do today? Tell me, tell me." Yatri shrugged and giggled.

"Come on, everyone, help me out here." I tugged on Draco's shirt. "Draaaaaaaaaco, you'll help me, won't you?" I whined. "Tell me, what should I do?"

The kids burst out laughing as Draco frantically tried to tuck his shirt in.

Shifting out of the role playing, I sat up straight in my chair and asked, "Is that what I do, writers, when I am not sure what to do?"

The children all chorused, "Nooooooo." I nodded and firmly agreed with them. "No way!"

Name the teaching point.

"Today I want to teach you that when writers have problems and don't know what to do, they say, 'I can solve this myself.' Then writers come up with solutions to those problems and carry on, writing, writing, writing. That way, writers don't waste precious time!"

♦ COACHING

- Pretend I don't know what to do on my garden paper

- annoyingly ask kids what I should do

- "Is that what I do when I'm not sure what to do?"

TEACHING

Demonstrate that you solve your own problems and figure out what to do during writing time.

"Let me show you what I mean." Resuming the role of the desperate and stuck writer, I said, "I finished my writing about the garden and I don't know what to do next. Who will help me decide? Will my mother tell me what to do? Should I call her up?" I got out my cell phone, acting out that possibility.

The kids shook their heads.

"Will the principal tell me what to do?" I started to get up to go to the office.

Again, the kids shook their heads.

Nodding, and sitting tall, I confirmed, "You are right. I am the writer, so I need to decide. It is like I am the boss of my own writing." Pulling out my page of writing, I looked it over with new sense of self-direction. "I'm the boss of this, so I get to say if it is done or not. Hmm, . . . I am looking to see if, one, I have a lot of information here about the garden, and I do. Two, I am looking to see if I filled up the page, and I did. Three, I am looking to see if my name is here, and it is. Four, I am looking to see if I got words on my page, and I see not that many. Only two.

"So, now I know what I am going to do. I am going to write more words, and then start a new page. The words are easy. I'll just say the words and write the sound I hear—but the new page?"

Resuming the role play of a needy writer, I beseeched a child, "Help me, Yatri. What do I write about? Help me, help me. Oh no, oh no . . ."

Yatri laughed and, with the class joining in, told me, "You gotta do it yourself!"

"You are right," I said, sitting tall. "And I can think of what I know about. Hmm, . . . What do my friends and I talk about. I know! I know about cooking nice food and having people come over to my house." I took out a new page out of the writing tray (one that usually sits at each one of the tables) and quickly put my name on the top. At that point, I stopped.

Debrief, emphasizing the way your realization that you can solve your problems pertains to other days and other children.

"Did you see what I did? When I was done with my garden piece and wasn't sure what to do, I didn't go line up beside the teacher for help. I didn't call my mother. Instead, I realized that I am the boss of my own writing, and I solved my own problem. I read over my writing, checking to see if it was done, and I realized I still gotta add more words. I'll do that soon. I also realized then that I should write another page. You, too, can be the boss of your writing and make your own decisions about what to do next. Remember, if you're not sure what to do, you can read over our 'When We Are Done, We Have Just Begun' chart. That can help give you ideas for what to do, too!"

- Briefly role-pl
- "I am the my own i
- "I didn' the pac words easy. Slow wri' I l
- I'll
- Briefly

"I can think about who
Oh! M
"Did y did?"
- Read our

. . . nonstration to . . . eel the different . . . the way your into- . . . After most demonstrations, there will be a time for you to debrief, and that's a time when you are no longer acting like a writer. You are the teacher who has been watching the demonstration and now turns to talk, eye to eye with kids, asking if they noticed this or that during the previous portion of the minilesson.

ACTIVE ENGAGEMENT

Quickly recap a couple of the "problems" you told children you were having earlier and recruit their help solving these.

"I was just playing around earlier when I pleaded for poor Yatri and Draco to help me. But let's pretend that I really am having those problems. Let's say that I'm ready to write a new book, but there's no more paper in my tray. Do I just stop writing? Do I just give up for the day? Do I line up behind the teacher and whine, 'Help me! Help me!' Or are there ways I might solve these problems? Turn and tell the person sitting next to you what I should do if there is no more paper in the tray.

"So, writers, I heard some of you say that I could go to another table that has paper in their tray! What problem solvers!

"What if my pen runs out of ink? Turn and talk quickly. What should I do?

"A lot of you said that I could get a new pen. Of course! There are lots of pens on the table, and if there aren't any left, I could always find one in the writing center. What a great solution!

"Last one, okay? What if I wrote piece and I don't like it and want to start a new one. What should I do? Just stop and not write anymore? Turn and talk, fast!

"*All* of you realized that there's tons of paper in the paper tray for me to use, so I *don't* need to give up on writing. I can just grab more paper and think about a new topic to write about. I can think about something else I know about and write about that!"

Debrief, reminding children that they are writers who come up with their own solutions for problems.

"Well, it's clear that you are *Super* Writers who can solve your own problems."

LINK

Channel students to expect that they'll encounter times when they don't know what to do. Remind them that when those times come, they have ways to "save the day."

"Writers, I have bad news. There will be problems today. Some of you will get stuck. You will sit there and think, 'I don't know what to do.'

"But I also have good news. The good news is that you are Super Writers, and you can 'save the day' and solve your own problems. I can't wait to see how you, the Super Writers, do that."

Writers, what if my pencil breaks, should I just give up?"

"what if I don't know how to write a letter?"

"what if I wrote a piece and I don't like it and want to start a new one. what should I do?"

"Spider writers," I think you're ready.

- *Bad news: there will be problems*

- *Good news: you can solve your own problems*

Problem Solving Management Concerns

BEFORE TODAY'S WORKSHOP, you can take a moment to anticipate the predictable challenges that you'll be addressing in your conferences and small-group instruction. Usually, the easiest way to think about this is to cluster students according to some of the most pressing issues and then to think about your goals for students who are facing those challenges.

You will inevitably have students who are so enthusiastic to begin writing that they forget, time and again, to write their name on their work. Pull this group together and say, "Last night I was admiring your work. I found this beautiful writing," showing a child's draft. "But then I thought, 'Who is the author?' Then I looked at the next piece of writing and I said, 'Wait! Who is the author of this one?' Soon I had a huge problem because I couldn't tell who the author was on almost any piece! Can you talk to your partner and see if we can invent a solution?" Chances are good that a child will suggest that writers add their names to their writing. A closer inspection will show that, in fact, published authors do just that!

You may also have a number of students who have taken you at your word when you encouraged them to write a second piece of writing. These youngsters will have been flying through a ream of paper, making a hasty scrawl on each page and then pronouncing it done. It may seem that writing their name and stamping the date has taken longer than any other part of writing. You may hold yourself in check, pleasantly asking these writers, "What are you making?" or "Can you read it to me?" Both of which are great responses because you are conveying your expectations. The youngster may not get the hint, however, and may earnestly point out that he is making new pieces. He may even count off the number of "completed" pieces. You will need to intervene. Don't rely on questions in an instance such as this. There is a place for clearly telling writers things they need to know. Tell these writers that the goal is to fill a page with information, making pages that will actually teach people a ton of stuff.

There will be students who are the opposite—who belabor the same piece for several days, adding additional layers to their text so that it almost looks as if one needs to do an archaeological dig to bring out all the meanings. You'll need to tell students that the goal is to make their writing into something that people can read and learn from. That means it is important to stop and move to another piece of paper once their page is full.

Another issue you may encounter in the early days of your writing workshop is students struggling when it comes to sharing community supplies. Not only are your students new to writing workshop, but many of them may be new to a structured school day or being part of a larger community of peers. It is not uncommon to hear children arguing over who gets to use the date stamp first or which one gets the purple marker. On the following page, you'll see how I go about helping two students.

MID-WORKSHOP TEACHING
The Sound of a Productive Writing Workshop

"Writers, Nicky just told me he couldn't think because of the noise, and Sebastian said *he* couldn't concentrate. That's a problem because all of you are writing really important information pieces, and you all need to be able to do your best work. I asked Sebastian and Nicky how they thought they might solve this big problem, and they had a great suggestion. Let's listen to them."

Nicky and Sebastian stood, chests puffed forward, and Nicky announced, dramatically, "We gotta all *whisper*."

I gave them a thumbs up and asked the class, "Are you willing to try? Are you willing to use two-inch voices?" To demonstrate, I whispered, "Like this?"

After a few minutes of children talking softly while they worked and me reminding the outliers, I said, "Writers, listen to how the room sounds. This is the sound of a good writing workshop. Now everyone can concentrate and do their best work."

As Students Continue Working . . .

"I see Fabian look at the chart and then start a new piece. He's writing his name already!"

"Super Writers, Yatri couldn't remember how to write *me*, but she looked up at the writing I have in the front of the room and it helped her write the word! She had a problem and solved it!"

"Owen couldn't remember what he wrote, but he didn't just sit there and say, 'Help me, help me.' No way! Owen touched everything in the picture, and that helped him remember what he put on his page."

"Margay couldn't think of what to write about next, so she looked around the room and decided to teach people about our library of books! She invented a brand-new strategy for coming up with ideas—looking around the room! Way to go, Super Writers! Keep your writing pens moving!"

As I was finishing up a conference with another student, I noticed an uproar at the red table and made that my next stop. Jordan and Ryan were halfway out of their chairs—each with a fist holding a blue marker and each doing his best to wrestle it away from the other. Most of the table's marker supply was spread out on the table in front of their seats.

"I don't see writers working here!" I exclaimed. "Where are the writers, Jordan and Ryan?" I knelt between them, breaking their eye contact. "Writers," I said seriously, "*do not* wrestle over markers. Can you imagine Mem Fox and Tomie DiPaola wrestling over markers?

"Boys, look at me." They turned. Jordan's eyes were wet and he was breathing hard, little fists clenched. Ryan looked determinedly at the floor. "Writers, I want you each to tell me what is happening here to keep you from your important writing work. Jordan, you first."

"He keeps on taking all the markers, and I need blue! He took all the blues!"

"*No!*" Ryan interrupted. "*He's* the one taking them! He wouldn't give me any before, so I just took them!"

I knew that I needed to step in and redirect these writers. I had to teach them about the expectations of a writing workshop. In this case, I needed to help them understand that writing time is for writing, and that a writing community shares supplies.

"Aha. Well, you *know* that I expect writers to be writing during writing workshop, not wrestling. I see that you're having trouble with the markers. I have a suggestion. When we keep the markers in the tub and just take out one when we need it, then *everybody* gets to use the markers. Every writer needs them to be able to add color and details to their pieces! So do that now. Put all the markers back in the tub. Remember, we always keep the markers in the tub and take out just the one we are using. The tub is always right here in the middle of the table so everyone can reach it." Reluctantly the boys plopped their hoarded markers back into the tub.

I then needed to help the boys move on. In this case, I needed to help them sit in spots where they could do their best work. "If it is not working for you two to be near each other today, find a smart spot away from each other. Writers sometimes need to move around a little bit to find a spot where they can do their best work. Where would you like to be today, Ryan, where you can do your very best work as a writer?" I asked this in a way as to signify that there was no other option but to move.

"I want to be on the rug with a clipboard," Ryan replied.

"Good choice. Go get yourself one, and I'll meet you over there in a few minutes to talk about your writing work! Jordan, will you be able to keep working at the table?" He nodded yes.

At this point I wanted to name what the children had done as writers and remind them to do this often in future writing. "So, boys, you're doing a good job remembering that our writing community shares supplies and that we help each other find smart places to do our best work. You can keep these things in your heads every day so that you won't have marker trouble during writing workshop. And guess what? It's exactly the same for the other supplies. We share them."

More Tools for the Writing Workshop
Writing Folders and Date Stamps

Engage children in helping you solve the problem of where to store ongoing and finished writing, setting up folders and the ritual of storing work in them.

"Writers, I want to congratulate you for carrying on so well all on your own. This room has the buzz of a productive workshop! Many of you started another piece today! Some of you have even started a third or a fourth or a fifth piece. This class is writing up a storm! But now we have a new problem. Where are we going to put all these pieces that we have made? I was talking with a few of you, and we came up with an idea. How about if you each have your own writing folder, like professional authors have? Your folder can be a little home for your writing." I distributed a folder to each child.

"Can I tell you about a little system that some kids in another school came up with to help organize their writing? These kindergartners decided they should put their finished work on this side (the left pocket) and the work they were still working on over here (the right pocket). To remember which pieces of writing were stopped, or done, they put a red stoplight (a red sticker) on the one side, and for pieces they still wanted to work on, they put a green 'go' light (a green sticker) on the other. The cool thing is that two five-year-olds came up with that system, and now thousands of kids all across the world are using that same system! You want to try it too?" The children decided yes, so I called on the table monitors to distribute large red and green dots.

Introduce date stamps and teach writers to date their work today and every day.

"Writers, before you slide your work carefully into a pocket, making sure it doesn't bunch up, I have one more system for you. I've put a date stamp on each of your tables. Please stamp today's date (it will always be set to the day's date) on each piece as you put it away, and after this, put this stamp on whatever you are working on every day."

> - Review blue folder procedure.
>
> - Introduce date stamp

FIG. 3–1   Shari's writing: *Elevator*

Session 4

Writers Call to Mind What They Want to Say, Then Put That onto the Page

IN THIS SESSION, you continue to teach children what it means to participate in the writing process. You will return to the instruction you have given children in generating ideas for writing, or rehearsal, and again return to the all-important message that writers get started working on a piece of writing by thinking of the content they want to record on the page. Writers have meanings to communicate and topics to teach.

This is an important message to teach very young children because otherwise, you will see that often when a child sits before a blank page and picks up a marker or pen to write, his first thought is, "What can I draw?" The child then begins by drawing the one thing that he has practiced drawing before: a house, a row of tulips, a fighter jet, a superhero. If you come alongside the child who is adding a picket fence to his picture of a house and ask the youngster why he has chosen that topic, what he wants to teach about houses, it may well turn out that this is a child who lives in a tall apartment building, who has no knowledge of or interest in houses.

The problem with children beginning to write by thinking, "What can I draw?" is not just that they may end up writing about topics they neither know nor care about. The problem is also that the process they are experiencing is not at all like what writers do. Writers have something to say, something in mind that needs to get onto the page.

If a youngster wants to teach all about supermarkets because he knows a lot about them, and if he begins writing by conjuring up a recent image of the store and then works industriously to put that image onto the page, returning to the image often to recall yet more details to add to the representation, that child's final product may look rather like the final product of the child who regarded writing time as an invitation to draw a house, but this second writer is engaged in something far closer to the writing process.

In this session, then, you will teach children that when writers get ready to write teaching (or informational) texts—when they rehearse for writing—they think about a topic they want to teach others. Writers begin writing by making a mental image of that topic, of whatever it is they want to say, and then work to capture that meaning on paper. Today you will ask students to close their eyes and picture something they want to put onto their paper and then make drawings that are representational.

IN THIS SESSION, you'll teach students that writers picture what they want to write about first and then put all of the details onto the page.

GETTING READY

- ✔ Chart paper and markers

- ✔ One child's work, enlarged to serve as a model for the minilesson

- ✔ A class topic (this book uses the school playground) that you and the children will add to together

- ✔ Student writing that demonstrates a writing strategy others could benefit from, or Aleysha's writing, in the online resources (see Share)

- ✔ *Naked Mole Rat Gets Dressed* by Mo Willems or another text that shows action through the illustrations (see Share)

Writers Call to Mind What They Want to Say, Then Put That onto the Page

CONNECTION

Tell about a child who pictured what she wanted to write before she began and then put this onto the page, using detailed illustrations. Show an enlarged version of her writing.

"Writers, yesterday, when I was watching Gabriela write (see Figure 4–1), I saw her close her eyes, and then she opened them and told me that she was going to write about supermarkets because she goes to the supermarket with her mom, dad, and sisters all the time and knows a lot about them. Here is the really cool thing: because Gabriela pictured that supermarket in her mind before writing about it, she added so many things to her page that can really help us as readers. Because Gabriela added so much, *we* can read her page and picture her supermarket in *our minds* as we read. Let's try it.

"I've enlarged Gabriela's writing so that all of you can read it with me. Let's look at her pictures and see if we can make a picture in our minds of the supermarket. Here, this is page one," I said, showing the page to the class.

"I'm looking at this picture, and I can see there are people at the supermarket, right? Can you tell how many people are at the supermarket? One, two, three! Yeah! And they are all in a line to buy food, right? Because Gabriela really pictured the people and thought, 'How many people are there? Where are they, exactly?' and then she put that information on her paper, so that we can read her paper and *we can picture that store*!

"Can you tell where the fruit stand is? It is next to this girl. And do you see the shopping cart? It is right near the cash register, isn't it? Gabriela even put some bananas in this cart, didn't she? And look, there is a *b* next to them. I think these are apples because they are round and they have an *a* next to them. Am I right, Gabriela?"

Gabriela smiled and nodded.

Occasionally, we spotlight particular children in the classroom whose actions or work model some aspect of the day's teaching that we hope other children will do. It's important that children feel "famous" now and then, and also that they learn from each other.

FIG. 4–1   Gabriela's writing: *This is the supermarket. There is food. These are the apples. We are in the checkout. This is the cart. Here are the bananas.* (Labels: *Apples. Bananas.*)

Debrief in a way that emphasizes the transferable work one writer has done that you hope others will do as well.

"Gabriela closed her eyes and pictured the supermarket with the people in a line and the fruit in a pile, and then she put the exact details of that picture onto her paper, didn't she? The more we can picture what we want to say, even the details, the more readers can picture it as well."

❖ **Name the teaching point.**

"Today I want to teach you that once writers have something they want to write about, it helps for them to get that topic—their garden, the supermarket—in mind before they write. Sometimes writers close their eyes, picture the topic they want to write about, and then put all the details into the picture and words."

TEACHING

Begin a piece of shared writing about a topic familiar to the children as well as to you. Model that you picture the topic, then record details, checking your mental image for more specifics.

"Writers, let's try to do what Gabriela did, only let's teach people about our playground instead of about supermarkets. Let's start by picturing the topic, the playground, so we can make our writing full of detailed information."

I closed my eyes, tilted my head skyward, very obviously conjuring up a mental image, and then said, "I can picture it! I can see *our playground* in my mind! I'm seeing the swings—there are three of them, only one has a broken seat. The seat hangs there, scraping the ground. I'm seeing a seesaw and about *ten kids* sitting on it!" I stopped and checked in with the kids. "Were you able to picture our topic, too?"

Not waiting for their input just yet, I used my hand to quell their talk and pressed on to the next part of the demonstration. "Now we've got to think, 'How can we put that on the paper?' Let me start with the seesaw. Hmm, . . . It looks like a long, straight line," I said, and made a long line on the chart paper. "It has little handles on each end. Hmm, . . . How do they look? Let me check."

I closed my eyes, referring back to the mental image, and then said, "They look like little half squares," and I drew the handles.

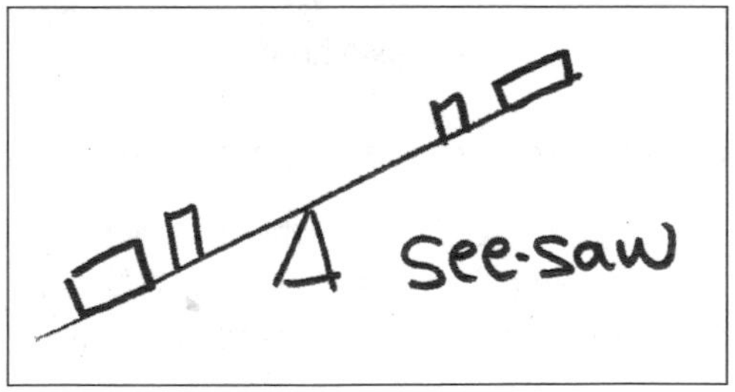

Debrief, reminding students how you visualized the details before you put them on the page.

I turned back to the class. "Do you see how I went back to the picture in my mind to figure out details we could put into our picture of the seesaw? Now we're going to have to figure out exactly how all those kids fit onto the seesaw and how they are holding on so we can put that in our writing as well."

As noted in Session 3, students will be aware when you shift from the demonstration to debriefing, just by your changes in tone and posture.

FIG. 4–2 Teacher's demonstration of the seesaw

ACTIVE ENGAGEMENT

Recruit the children to continue the work of envisioning the playground and then drawing with imaginary pens on the carpet, showing what they'd add to the class writing.

"I'll finish the seesaw in a minute, but let's work together on something else that is on our playground. Let's try the slide. Close your eyes. Picture the slide in your mind. What shape is it? How could you draw it? What do you notice about it?"

After a few seconds of silence, I said, "Now, let's imagine that we are going to draw the slide, only with imaginary markers! Turn to the person next to you and, with an imaginary marker, show your friend what you think is important for people to know about the slide. Draw with our imaginary markers on the imaginary paper of our carpet, and tell about what you are drawing, too."

Recruit one writer to share the content he pretended to draw, adding it to the shared writing, and then channel him to label with a word or two.

After letting them do this for a few seconds, I called on one child. "Fabian, what do you notice about the slide that you could put onto the paper (or the pretend paper)?"

With his eyes still closed, Fabian squinted, as if trying to get a closer look at the slide. He moved his hand around in a spiral-like fashion and said, "It is a curvy line coming down."

"It isn't a straight slide? It spirals round and round?" I confirmed. "That's an important detail. Fabian, come up and add that to our writing about the playground, okay?" He did that, drawing a person on the top of the slide. When I asked who that was, Fabian said he'd drawn a picture of himself. I said to the rest of the class, "And let's write, 'Fabian' next to the picture so we know that is Fabian, okay? To do that, class, say the word really slowly, listening for the first sound. Let's do it together." The class chimed in to say, "Fffffabian," and some children called out "F," which Fabian wrote. He then went on to complete his name.

FIG. 4–3   Fabian's addition of a spiral slide to the class's playground picture, signed with his name.

Rally the whole class to generate ideas for places they could label the pictures in the class text.

"Class, what else could we label in our writing about the slide? Tell the person beside you." The room buzzed for a few seconds before I reconvened the class. "I heard we could add, *fast* and *curvy* and *high!* You have a ton of things we could write, but for now, we need to save time for you to get started on your own work."

LINK

Remind students not only of today's teaching point, but of the cumulative lessons learned so far. Channel them to be problem solvers, to remember to reread and add on, and to envision before writing or revising.

"Of course, today and every day you are going to work on your own writing, not on our class writing about the playground. Remember all that you have learned so far this year about being writers, okay? I'll say something I hope you have learned, and will you give me a thumbs up if you *already knew* the thing that I am saying?

"Here's one thing: writers think about things we know about, that we can teach others, and then make pieces to teach people about those things. Did you already know that?" Children nodded, and with a thumbs up signaled that they'd heard this before.

"How about this one? When writers are finished with a piece of writing, we don't just say, 'I'm done.' Instead writers have a saying: 'When I'm done, I've just begun.' Writers finish a piece, and they look back and think, 'What can I add on?'" Many children showed that they knew this.

"How about this? When writers want to come up with ideas for what to draw and write, we sometimes close our eyes and picture whatever it is we are writing about, then we put that picture onto the page." The children all signaled that, absolutely, they already knew this.

"Let's get ready to write, right here and now! Think about what you are going to write about today. It might be adding onto a piece you have started, or it might be a new piece. When you have decided on your topic, close your eyes. Once you have your subject in mind, open your eyes and signal with a thumbs up that you're ready to write." As children signaled, I motioned for them to head to their writing spots and get started.

This kind of link is one you might use over and over, as needed. Remind children of all they know, and make sure they remember to not just do the work taught in the minilesson, but to do exactly the work they need to do in order to write well and follow their own purposes.

FIG. 4–4 Fabian's writing: *This is my brother. This is breakfast. Here is the bowl of cereal. It is granola. Here is the juice with a straw.* (Labels: *Brother. Shirt. Buttons.*)

Study Your Students' Writing to Gain Insights for Future Teaching

THE WRITING WORKSHOP provides us with an amazing window into our children's understandings of written language. After even just one day in the writing workshop, we can bring our children's writing home and pore over it. Each piece of writing helps us develop a theory of the writer and his or her knowledge of literacy.

Margay, for example, relies on a few high-frequency words (see Figure 4–5). I will be interested to see if this is a pattern. I'm interested that she has fearlessly tackled words such as *read*, *draw*, and *spell*, representing each sound (including the vowels) with a letter. She seems able to invent spellings but may be hesitant to do so. I notice that her text is brief for someone with her skills. What would her writing have been like if she did it on lined paper? I plan to nudge her to write more.

When Ryan colored in his whole picture space (see Figure 4–6), was he trying to represent nighttime? On the lines, he copied the alphabet. I wonder what he would say he has done. I will ask, "What's your writing about?" or "Will you read me your writing?" to learn whether he believes his print carries meaning. I plan to suggest we write something together and then elicit some content from him. Then I'll ask him to write the first word, and I'll learn more about this mystery.

Sebastian's drawing seems to contain a whole drama (see Figure 4–7). He seems to care that his ideas come across to readers. I don't know if this is one person in lots of situations or if it's a lot of different people in a sort of tableau. I think I recognize various playground activities, but Sebastian will have to help me understand what I am

FIG. 4–5   Margay's writing: *I can write. I can read. I can spell. I can draw. I can do math.*

FIG. 4–6   Ryan has put something he knows a lot about—the alphabet—onto his paper.

FIG. 4–7   Sebastian's detailed drawing reveals much about how he approaches writing. He seems to care that his ideas come across to readers.

"Writers, eyes up here." I waited, giving the room a 360-degree scan. "Writers, sometimes we are wasting precious writing time because after I ask you to look up here, some of you keep writing. I know you don't want to stop working, but we need a way for me to give you a quick tip. Some kids in one school invented a plan that worked for them. Can I teach it to you and see if you like it?

"What happens is, I sing, 'Stop, look, and listen,' and then you, hearing this, stop what you are doing, look at me, and freeze. Once you have done that, and you are frozen, you sing back, 'Oh yeah,' as a way of saying, 'We are ready to listen.'

"Are you willing to try this? If so, get back to work, and forget about me for a minute." After sixty seconds, I sang out, "Stop, look, and listen," and then the children stopped, froze, looked at me, and sang back, "Oh yeah!"

This time I continued with the mid-workshop teaching point. "I want to show you what Hailey is doing as a writer. Hailey is writing about the beach, so she drew the ocean. Do you see it here? And then Hailey did something really smart. She thought about what *else* she could teach us about the beach. Not just the ocean! She began to make sea shells and palm trees too! Writers, when you are teaching, try to do what Hailey did. Think about what *else* you could teach so that you really fill up your page, teaching us about *all* that you know about your topic!"

As Students Continue Working . . .

"Oh my gosh, writers, may I stop all of you? Derrick is drawing a picture of how his cat's whiskers tickled his belly in the bathtub. He says whiskers are hard for him to draw. I just know he is going to do it the best he can. Oh my gosh, Derrick is doing it. He is drawing the whiskers the best he can!"

"Don't just imagine one thing about your topic. Try to draw *many* things, like we started to do in the playground piece."

"I see Deja trying to remember what presents look like. She is using her imaginary marker (her finger) first to imagine the shape of the ribbon and then she is drawing it! Don't forget—really picture what you are teaching."

"If you are not sure what to do next, remember, you can add more information to your page or you can start a new piece."

seeing. I wonder what Sebastian will do when I ask, "Will you read me your writing?" I wonder if he thinks he has written a story or a teaching book, or if he regards this as only the illustration and plans to write a text.

By now, many of your children should be carrying on with their work well enough for you to engage in some one-to-one conferences, which will, in turn, give you an idea for some of the small-group work you might lead and for some content you can add to your whole-class teaching. That is, one-to-one conferences not only teach the writer, but they also teach you, and these conferences give even your whole-group teaching more traction.

In a good conference, you take lessons from the child first on whatever it is that he or she has chosen to write about—on the content of the child's writing—and on the

child's intentions and processes as a writer. During these early days of a writing workshop, when you are trying to teach children that their marks on the page communicate meaning to interested readers, first focus on listening to the child's content. The force of your attention will ignite the child's work.

So, start by hearing what it is that child has written. The text could appear to be a scrawled drawing with no hint of letters, and you'll still ask the writer to read you the writing. As you listen, keep in mind times in your own life when someone has listened well to you. Chances are that the people who listen really responsively end up getting you to say more than you would have said—or thought—had the responsive listener not been there. Be *that* kind of listener, but keep in mind that listening can be responsive, yet also brief. Get used to the rhythm of listening for a minute or two and then letting your conference bend toward the goal of helping the writer do more.

Showing Action in Pictures

Use one student's piece of writing to demonstrate a strategy that others could benefit from as well. In this case, teach children that their drawings can depict actions.

"Stop, look, and listen," I sang, and the children froze and sang back, "Oh yeah." Once they were looking at me quietly, I orchestrated a way for children from different tables to come quickly to the meeting area, keeping Aleysha near me at the front of the meeting area. Once the children had convened, I began. "Writers, I noticed Aleysha doing something today that we can all learn from. Aleysha decided she wanted to teach people not only what things there are to do at recess, but also *how* they do things."

Aleysha held her paper high as if showing it to the class, and said, "They are jumping rope," pointing to a picture of two kids jumping (see Figure 4–8).

"Class, what was interesting to me is that Aleysha added these little lines under each foot." I pointed to three action marks under each foot. Aleysha explained that they were action marks, and I nodded. "After I saw these in Aleysha's book, I checked out some books by published authors, and I saw that some of those books use marks a lot like Aleysha's to show action. Like, look at this book by Mo Willems," I said, and showed the class a page from *Naked Mole Rat Gets Dressed*. "Aleysha loves this book, and so do I. Maybe I'll read it aloud later and we can look at how Mo uses action marks. But for right now, think about whether anyone or anything in *your* picture is in action—is running or jumping or driving—and if there is a place where you could add action marks. Show the person beside you where that is. Turn and talk."

Children talked, and then I said, "We've got two minutes to pack up. Show me that you remember what to do to put your writing, your markers, your pens—the works—away! Get started."

If you don't see any examples of this in your class' writing, feel free to use Aleysha's work—we've also put it in the online resources for you. Or, you could use your own work. You might even ask the class to invent a way to depict how people do things.

FIG. 4–8 Aleysha's writing: *Jump high. I am teaching people about jump rope.* (Labels: *Jumping. Rope. Floor.*)

Stretching Out Words to Write Them

Y OU WILL HAVE NOTICED that prior to now, we have referred to children's work as *writing* when actually, for many children, there has not been a lot of writing at all. Today that will change. Your message will be, "Writers write with pictures *and* words."

This session helps students develop phonemic awareness and begin to build toward conventional reading and writing. Most state standards call for kindergarten students to be able to spell simple words phonetically, using what they know about letter-sound correspondence, and to put spaces between words. They must also be able to isolate and pronounce all the sounds in a CVC (consonant-vowel-consonant) word and read common high-frequency words with automaticity. This unit is a first step toward meeting these standards. Of course, your diverse group of spellers will represent a wide range of understandings about letters, sounds, and words.

Some valuable instructional resources and materials for word study are the *Words Their Way* series by Donald Bear, Marcia Invernizzi, and Shane Templeton and *Phonics Lessons* by Irene C. Fountas and Gay Su Pinnell. If you are using a resource like these, you have probably begun analyzing your students' knowledge of word features (letters, spelling patterns) and the ways they use word-solving strategies when they write words. You have probably administered an assessment to find out how many letter names and sounds your students know. If this showed that some children know most of their letter sounds, you will also want to administer a spelling inventory. By looking at the information provided by assessments like these and also by studying your students' writing and spelling behaviors, you will see what they already know. Understanding their strengths will help you determine where to begin your word study instruction.

You'll teach youngsters that writers slowly say whatever it is they want to write, listening for the first sound, then use the letters of the alphabet to record that sound. Don't worry whether your children know the alphabet or have a command of letter-sound correspondence. This lesson will be just as important for children who do not yet know any letter-sound correspondence as it will be for the children who spell sight words correctly.

IN THIS SESSION, you'll teach students that young writers say words slowly and then write down the sounds that they hear.

GETTING READY

- ✔ One child's work that will serve as a model for the minilesson

- ✔ Enlarged name chart with each child's name printed next to the letter with which it begins. Children should already be familiar with this chart.

- ✔ Class piece of shared writing and markers (see Teaching and Active Engagement)

- ✔ "When We Are Done We Have Just Begun" chart (see Mid-Workshop Teaching)

- ✔ Copy of name chart for each child to have on hand while writing

Most children are dying to write letters and happy to approximate as best they can. Their writing may end up looking like a chicken stepped in ink and then ran across the page, but the writers will be proud as punch that they've written some words.

"Most children are dying to write letters and happy to approximate as best they can."

In this lesson, you'll teach children that writers say the word they want to write. They say it slowly, often repeatedly, listening for the initial sound. Do this with a word that has an easy-to-identify initial sound. For example, *m* can be stretched out like a rubber band, with that sound continuing on and on. Then too, the names of some letters (*m, s, r, l, n*) all carry the sound they make, making sound-letter correspondence easier. If you want to spell *me* and recall that the double-mountain shape is an *m*, then putting those together is not all that hard! And given that most of the drawings a kindergarten child will make will feature themselves, teaching children to hear and record *m* is a lesson that will pay off!

Your bigger point will be that children can listen and record all the sounds in the words they want to write, and of course many of your children won't yet know all their sound-letter correspondence. Some children, then, will isolate the initial sound and then need to ask a friend, "How do you spell /rrrrr/?" Or, alternatively, the child may just record a diamond or a lollipop-like mark in lieu of a letter. Either way, this is still extremely important work for this child to do because isolating and hearing sounds is an essential part of developing phonemic awareness skills.

Stretching Out Words to Write Them

CONNECTION

◆ COACHING

Find a way to elicit and celebrate the topics writers are writing about, and use this as a way to convey your interest in learning from their areas of expertise.

"Super Writers, wow! You are teaching so much through your books. How about we quickly share our topics with everyone in this room—want to do that?" The kids bobbed their heads yes.

Even as we focus on the mechanics and conventions of writing, we need to be sure to balance that with an enthusiasm for the content and meaning of writing.

"I'm going to tap one of you, then another, then another, lightly on the head, and when I tap you, will you tell everyone what one of your teaching books is about? Say it in just a few words, like 'my family' or 'horses.'"

I tapped Sophie and she said, "My family." Then I tapped Owen who sang out, "My dinosaur puzzle." Yatri jumped up on her knees and said, "Magic tricks!" And this continued for a few more children.

Tell the story of being stalled when trying to read a child's writing at home because pictures weren't labeled. Explain that the writer later added labels that clarified everything.

"Writers, you are all writing on such interesting topics that I am *dying* to read your books. Ryan has a really interesting topic. He is teaching us all about his family. I always read right before I go to sleep, so last night, I turned on my reading light and snuggled down to read about Ryan's family. I started to read, and saw this." I showed the children a picture Ryan had drawn. "'Hmm,' I thought. 'I wonder who this is. It is a guy with huge furry hair, and I was dying to know who had that hair. Lying there in my bed with Ryan's writing, I thought, 'Is this Ryan's dad? Is it his brother? Who?'"

This connection also serves to help children learn from each other what they might write about next.

"Writers, when I got to school, Ryan said it was his dad—and you know what he did? He picked up his pen and wrote that—'Dad'—beside the picture. So, now any one of you can take his writing home, and you will know what you are looking at. He also wrote 'suitcase' beside this thing the guy with the furry hair was holding. I thought the guy was holding a huge chunk of dirt but it turns out it is a suitcase!"

Transition toward setting up today's lesson on getting words onto the page.

"We know that writers write words the best they can. So when I saw that some of you hadn't written any words, I thought to myself, 'Wait a sec. Maybe it's *my* fault if some of you aren't getting down enough words. Maybe I haven't taught you enough ways to actually get words onto the page.' So listen up, because this is important."

❖ Name the teaching point.

"Today I want to teach you that writers use words as well as pictures to teach people what we know. Writers write words by saying the word slooooooowwwwwwwwwly and then writing down the first sound they hear."

TEACHING

Compare sounding out words to stretching out a rubber band, and get children stretching out words that you and they need to add to the class text.

"Have you ever tried stretching a rubber band as far as it will go? You stretch it out nice and slow, like this," I held a rubber band between my fingers to demonstrate. "Guess what, writers! It's the same thing with words! When you are trying to write words, it can help to stretch them out nice and slow so that you can hear all the sounds and get those onto the page. Watch me while I do that.

"Let's look at our playground writing and see what words we could add. Oh! We should write 'monkey bars.'

"*Monkey bars* is a lot to write! Let's say it slowly together and then watch how I figure out what to write: monkey bars. Monkey bars. Mmmmm." As we all said the word slowly, the children and I mimicked that we were holding a rubber band, stretching it out farther and farther. "Mmmmmm. /m/. That's like *me* and . . . what else? Let's think if there is anyone in this class whose name starts with /m/. We can look at the name chart, too."

Margay, meanwhile, had jumped to her feet. "You are right. Mmmmargay. And Mmmatthew! Point to your names on the name chart." They did, and I concluded, "So *monkey bars* starts like *Margay* and *Matthew*, with an *m*." I recorded the letter beside the picture.

"Class, did you see how we stretched out the word *monkey bars*, listening for the sound we heard first, and then we wrote that sound? Let's keep going, and see if we hear any other sounds in *monkey bars*. Monkkkkkk."

I was not sure that many children in the class would hear any internal sounds, so this was experimental. A child or two made /k/ noises, so I nodded and quickly recorded that, but then decided to move on, giving children practice hearing more first sounds.

It is important that by October, each of your kindergartners will at least grasp the principle that each sound (or phoneme) needs to be represented with at least one letter (or letter-like mark) on the page. This is foundational, and even children who do not yet have a strong knowledge of letter-sound correspondence can learn this principle. You will also see that in short order, with strong instruction, more and more of your children will move from using letter-like marks to using letters. Once you have begun some work with phonics and taught or reminded children of letter names, you will see them using their beginning knowledge of letters and sounds as they write. When a child writes the word coat, he might record a c or k for the initial sound, and if the child hears an ending sound, he might use either a t or d to capture it. These sorts of spellings are expected for kindergartners.

Debrief. Remind students of what they saw you do and why it is helpful.

"Writers, thank goodness we labeled those monkey bars, 'cause I'm not the best drawer. But now that we have labels, anyone can read our writing and know what we've got on our playground. Did you notice how I listened to the sounds and thought about how the word started? I think you could all do that, too!"

ACTIVE ENGAGEMENT

Channel students to work on labeling another item in the class text, again stretching the word out slowly and hearing constituent sounds.

"Let's try labeling something else in our writing. How about this?" I pointed to the sun, and soon children were working with partners to say "sun" slowly, stretching out the first sound. "Sssssssss. What sound do you hear? /S/ like . . . ," and children began producing names from the class list.

"Listen to the way you are saying the word slooooowly! I hear lots of you saying your words like you're stretching out a rubber band. I hear you saying 'ssssssun' like Sssssssophie and Sssssssabastian. Liam just realized that ssssssssun begins like ssssssslide and sssssswings, two other items we put on our playground piece. You're really getting the hang of this, writers."

LINK

Send students off to write, equipping them with name charts and with resolve to write as well as to draw.

"Writers, today I know you will be doing all that we learned. How many of you are going to picture whatever you are writing about, so you can add little details to your writing?" They signaled that they were.

"Great. And how many of you are going to write words to label things in your writing?" They signaled that they were.

"Great. I've put little name charts next to each of your writing spots so that you can use that to help you write. So, remember to stretch out your words slooooooowly to really hear the sounds, and then check the name chart to see if it can help. Are you ready for this challenge? Are you ready to do some hard work!? Off you go!"

The important thing in this session is that you expect children's drawings and spellings, both, to change visibly and quickly and to do so right away. Just as you should expect children's drawings to become representational so that by October a house will have some resemblance to a house, you can also expect that children will begin to label half a dozen objects on each page. The labels will be composed of letter-like shapes that go left to right, but more writers will use a bunch of consonant letters to represent first or dominant sounds in words.

Supporting Students in Getting Words on Their Papers

THE WORK YOU HAVE TAUGHT in your minilesson is work that really is best taught through one-to-one conferences. It is great to rally kids to think about adding words to their pictures, but you really need to pull your chair alongside youngsters and make it happen. Essentially, what you need to do is teach like crazy. If a child draws himself on a bike, when you pull close to that child, listen to what he wants to write ("I rode my bike."), and then point to the part of the drawing that resembles a bike and say, "Let's write *bike*." If the child protests that he does not know how to write *bike*, then tell him, "I'll show you how. First, say *bike* slowly. Do that." Let him do it on his own. If you sense he needs support, join him, speaking in a quieter voice than his.

Then say, "Let's think about what sounds we hear in b . . . i . . . k . . . ," and say it with him again, this time more slowly. "Say it with me," you'll say again, so the child joins you in saying the word in a stretched out fashion. Listen with the child to the sounds as he articulates the word. "What do you hear?" The child might say, "I hear a *b*," but it is as likely that he will say, "I hear /b/," in which case you will tell him, "Write that down," and then look intently at the paper, as if you have not a single doubt that he can supply the letter. It is interesting to see what the child produces. In Draco's piece about pizza, he was able to hear and record one or two sounds in a few words (see Figure 5–1). You will want to make sure that students similar to Draco are able to carry on independently. To do so, looking at their work will not be enough. You will also have to teach students as they practice saying and recording letters across their books.

After setting the child up to record the sound, you need to look at the paper. You will feel the child's eyes fixed on you, as if he is saying, "How and what do I write?" The normal tendency, when you feel someone looking beseechingly at you, is to meet that person's eyes. Don't do it. Just continue staring at the place on the page where you anticipate the child will soon write, saying, "Just stick it here." Eventually, the child is apt to shrug and then to make some sort of a mark.

If the child records anything, even if the mark is a wiggle and not a letter, read it back, /b/, joining the child in reading /b/, and then making the long /i/ sound as the child

FIG. 5–1   Draco's writing: *This is lunch food.* (Labels: *Pizza. Table. Legs. Pepperoni pizza.*)

MID-WORKSHOP TEACHING
Reading Our Writing to Our Friends

"Stop, look, and listen," I sang out. "Oh yeah!" the students responded. "Writers, it seems to me that once you are writing with pictures *and* words, you all become not just writers, but also readers. Right now, take out your pointing finger. In a minute, I'm going to ask you to point to and read the pictures and then the words in your writing. Read this to yourself. Keep moving your finger and find something else on the page to read." Children did this.

"Now, read your writing to your friend who is sitting next to you. Decide who will go first, quickly. And then point to and read your pictures and words. Put your finger right *under* the word you are reading." They did this.

"Now read your writing to the person across from you." After children did this for a minute, I interrupted to say, "Wow, writers! You are also readers! I think I'm going to have to add 'We can reread our writing' to our "When We Are Done, We Have Just Begun" chart! Keep going! Let's write more so that we can read *more* of our writing to our friends! Go!"

"I can't hear you, writers! Pick something on your page and say the word slowly listening to all the sounds! Then write the letters the best you can! Let me hear you stretch them out!"

"I see Zoe looking around the room. She found the word *door* on our door—and labeled the door on her dollhouse that she is teaching us about! Use the room to help you! Another great strategy discovered by one of the Super Writers!"

"Don't just label one thing on your page. Try to label all the pictures on the page! Move your pen right now and tap all the things in your pictures that you could write a word next to!"

"I see you are working hard to say words and hear their sounds. Keep it up!"

prepares to record whatever he hears next. Again, nudge the child to record a mark representing that next sound.

If, on the other hand, the child did not isolate and hear a /b/ sound, you'll want to demonstrate how you say the word slowly and listen to a sound, producing your own /b/. You can also tell the child that the letter *b* makes a /b/ sound without feeling as if you are doing too much of the important work for the child because the most important lessons for the beginner revolve around phonemic awareness. Words can be said slowly; constituent sounds can be isolated and heard and then recorded. At the start of kindergarten, many children will need your help in saying words slowly, isolating the first sound, and making a mark on the page to represent that sound.

If the child has not isolated the first sound, you probably won't progress to help the child isolate and make marks representing later sounds. Instead you might move to asking the child to help you label other items—the sun, the child himself or herself. In each instance, help the child say the name of the item slowly, listening for the first sound and then making a mark to represent that sound. At this early stage, it is not essential that the mark be a letter, let alone that it be the correct letter!

In addition to one-to-one conferences, you may want to support labeling by leading a small-group session or two of interactive writing. To do this, cluster a few children together and recruit them to work together to help on a single piece of writing. It could be the class text or one child's text. Encourage the children in the small group to practice slowly saying the word that the writer wants recorded, listening for each sound, and to then write the words that match the pictures. Once children hear the first sound in a word, they might need to search for a letter or be taught how to use their alphabet chart to help them find the letter that makes the sound they heard and felt. You might label one page of your writing one day, putting six labels on the page. Interactive writing will give you a nice place to tuck in some of the state standards instruction that you'll be supporting across the year, including coaching children in the use of uppercase and lowercase letters.

In this session you gave children a name chart. In every unit of study, you will introduce a tool or two that remains throughout the rest of the year, often as a physical embodiment of the skill. In this minilesson, then, you not only gave children a name chart, but you also began the important work of reaching toward conventional spelling.

Adding Labels to Pictures

Channel children to reread what they have written to a friend, showing the new words and details they've added. Then remind them to store writing in their folders.

"Before you come over to the meeting area for the share, just to your friend next to you, will you read all the new words and information you added to your pieces? Don't forget to put your finger on the words you are reading."

After children did this for a minute, I sang out, "Stop, look, and listen," and waited for the children to sing the chorus, "Oh yeah."

"Writers, put your writing in your folder. Remember that if you are done, put that writing in the red dot side. If you still have some information that you need to add to the pictures and words, place it on the green dot side. Then put your folder into the caddy at your table. Let me see which tables are ready to come over to the meeting area."

Recruit children to help you use an imaginary pen to record words generated earlier to accompany the drawing of a slide, saying those words slowly. Make clear the expectation to write lots of words.

Soon the children were sitting in the meeting area. "I wanted us to meet here because I thought we might work together to be sure we had added *many* words to our class piece about the playground! Let's do some of this challenging work together! What else do we want to label about the slide? Let's try to remember what we wanted to say. Quickly tell your partner again the different words we should write.

"I heard you say we should write, *curvy*, *fast*, and *high!* I remember now! So let's start with *curvy*. Take out your imaginary rubber bands, and let's say it slooooooowly. /Cccc/ like *cat*, like *cookie*, like . . ." Look at the name chart and point to the picture on the name chart with the same sound. "Clarissa!" all the kids cheered! "And . . ." Point to the other picture. "Casey!" Great! Now, with your imaginary markers, take your finger and draw the letter *c* on the carpet! I'll put it right here next to the slide to show *curvy*. Say *curvy* one more time. Curveeeeeeeeeeeee."

"E! E!" Tanisa shouted. "I wrote the *e*."

"Let's read back what we have so far. Monkey bars. Sun. Slide. Swings. Curvy. Wow, we are writing lots of words!"

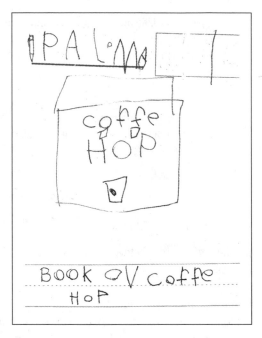

FIG. 5–2   Paloma's writing: *Coffee Shop, Book of Coffee Shops*

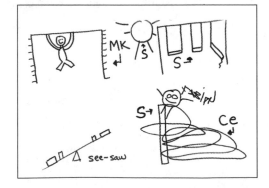

FIG. 5–3   Adding words to the class's playground piece. *Monkey bars. Sun. Slide. Swings. Curvy.*

Writing Even Hard-to-Write Ideas

TODAY, YOU'LL CONTINUE the theme of helping children persevere in the face of difficulty. Because you have worked on spelling as well as on drawing with detail, you'll now bring both of those together in one minilesson, suggesting that it is a sad day when a writer doesn't write what she wants to say because of worry that something is hard to draw or to spell. The minilesson, then, ostensibly addresses the times when children feel stuck because they can't draw or spell what they have in mind, but actually it is an effort to support resourcefulness and risk taking.

We will introduce the concepts of writing bravery and perseverance in this minilesson, but these qualities are not learned overnight; many students will take longer than a day to internalize them. Little by little, as you offer support and encouragement, students will take more risks. Your response to their approximations is vital. Even the tiniest note of criticism can send some children right back to square one. Be on the lookout, then, for things to compliment, and always pay the compliment with enthusiasm and sincerity before you start to address any needs.

You'll notice that the minilesson is a bit different than others have been. Instead of demonstrating a concept, using the class piece that has woven its way through the unit, you begin by retelling a familiar story, *The Little Engine that Could*, and then you progress toward some shared writing, done on white boards. It is helpful to guard against minilessons becoming so predictable that they are dull, so when you worry that some extra flavor is needed, it is helpful to remember that you can rely on the wisdom of published authors, using their writing to spice up your teaching. You aren't in this alone—every published author can be a teacher of writing with you!

IN THIS SESSION, you'll teach students that when writers have an idea that is hard to draw or a word that is hard to spell, they don't quit. Writers keep trying.

GETTING READY

✔ Your own writing and marker

✔ Prepared, focused, teaching book in your mind, ready to discuss with children

✔ "When We Are Done, We Have Just Begun" chart (see Mid-Workshop Teaching)

✔ Student piece of writing to demonstrate another way to draw and/or write difficult things (see Share)

✔ White boards and dry erase markers, one for each student (see Active Engagement)

✔ *Naked Mole Rat Gets Dressed* by Mo Willems or any other book that shows action through illustrations (see Share)

Writing Even Hard-to Write Ideas

CONNECTION

Tell children that you sometimes see them give up because they aren't sure how to write or draw the subject.

"Writers, I have been so excited about the things that you have been talking and writing about. But sometimes I see you excited about a great topic and then you go back to your seats and you're not sure how to draw the picture or write the words. And," I frowned sadly, "some of you, *actually decide not to tell* about your great topic because you aren't sure how to draw or spell it! That is *so sad* because the world misses out on your wonderful idea."

❖ Name the teaching point.

"Writers, you're not alone. I get the 'oh-no' feeling, and so do writers the world over. Today I want to teach you that when writers get that 'oh-no!' feeling about an idea that is hard, they don't just quit. They keep trying."

TEACHING

Tell a familiar tale that teaches the lesson that it's important to persist in the face of difficulties.

"Writers, have any of you ever heard the story of *The Little Engine That Could*? That story can teach us what we can do when we have that 'oh-no' feeling 'cause we don't know how to spell a hard word or how to draw a hard picture. That story can remind us not to give up.

"The story—some of you will remember—goes like this. There is a train that is full of toys for good little boys and girls. It is trying to go over the mountain, but it needs help. The Little Blue Engine is small, and she's never been over the mountain before, but she's brave. She says she'll help the other train.

"So she chugs along. Chugga chug chug, chugga, chug, chug. Toot toot! Toot toot! (Be the train with me.) Chugga chug chug, chugga chug chug. Toot toot! Toot toot! When the mountain gets steep, she doesn't say, 'This is too hard for me. I can't get over this whole mountain.' No way. She remembers all those little boys and girls, waiting on the other side, and she says, 'I think I can. I think I can. I think I can.' And you know what? Pretty soon that little train makes it over the top!"

◆ COACHING

Always, in a writing workshop, it's important to teach both the work that a writer does, and the habits a writer maintains. This session focuses on one essential habit of writers—continuing on, even when the going gets tough. We cannot overemphasize how important this seemingly simple message is, especially at the start of children's journey as writers. Above all, we want to encourage children to take risks as they work, embracing these as part of the writing process.

Debrief, rallying kids to persist when they encounter trouble.

"So, writers, when that train got to hard parts, when she thought, 'This is too hard,' did she give up? No way. Instead she said, 'I think I can, I think I can,' and she kept going. We can be like that when we are writing, too."

ACTIVE ENGAGEMENT

Recruit students to help you work through the hard parts of your writing, through interactive writing.

"Writers, I've been writing about gymnastics, and I've come to some hard parts. Will you help me? I'm going to give each of you a white board and a marker pen." I distributed these. "In my page about gymnastics, I was trying to draw someone standing on their hands. But whoa! That is *hard* to draw! I was ready to give up, but then I remembered that train, going over the mountain, saying," and the kids joined me for the refrain, 'I think I can, I think I can.'

"Everyone, take the caps off your marker pens! Will you try drawing someone doing a headstand?" I gave them a second to get started. "Who is thinking, 'Oh no! That's too hard?'" No one said anything. "None of you! You are really learning lessons from that little train." I let the children work for a minute, then said, "When you are done, put your caps on and hold up your boards! I see circles. Those are the peoples' heads? Look around. You all saw it differently, but you all tried! No one gave up! Amazing. Now wipe off your boards.

"Let's say that I wanted to write about the balance beam! *Balance* is a really hard word. Maybe we should just give up."

The kids, of course, said "Noooo!" and soon everyone was spelling that word on their white boards as well. "I see kids writing the letter *b* for bbbbalance! Great! Say the whole word: balaaaaaannnnce!" Afterward, I again said, "Hold up your boards! Wonderful! Now erase."

LINK

Remind students that you expect they will draw their own pictures the best they can.

"So, writers, I'm hoping that today and always when you are writing, if you think about something important to put into your teaching book, but it seems tricky to draw or write, then you will say to yourself, 'I think I can.' This work is not easy. We don't want *easy* work. We need a challenge! Do the best you can and do not give up! Off you go!"

If your children really enjoy doing a bit of writing on white boards, you may decide to do this more often. Always watch for your children's levels of engagement, and be ready to revise and refine your teaching plans based on what you know about your students.

Empowering Early Writers

FOR THE LAST FEW DAYS you have been trying to help your students come up with ideas, flesh out the details, and then get both pictures and words onto the page. Today's minilesson addressed a challenge that frequently arises in the early days of writing workshop: your students *have* ideas, they *have* pictured their ideas in their minds, and they *have* fleshed out the details. When it is time to put marker to paper, they may be afraid of "doing it wrong" or "not knowing how." A big part of your job as a teacher of writing, then, is to help your students become risk takers. Help them move beyond writing only about their mom because they know how to spell *mom.*

Nudge them to write about all the things that matter to them, even when they are hard to draw or spell accurately.

Teaching writing can feel a lot like spinning plates. We turn our focus from generating topics to internalizing routines to spelling to talking through an idea and so on. During this session, you supported children's bravery and persistence in spelling. Keep that plate spinning, but don't neglect the others. The information continuum will help you understand what some of those plates are. Study your students' work next to the

MID-WORKSHOP TEACHING   Using the "When We Are Done, We Have Just Begun" Chart

"Writers, I see many of you doing the best you can! I want to remind you about some things you can do when you think you might be done. Let's look at our 'When We Are Done, We've Just Begun' chart. It says, 'We can add to our pictures. We can add to our words. We can start a new piece. We reread our writing.' Will you read our chart with me?"

Students read the title and the items on the chart as I pointed to the words. "Look right now at the page you are working on. Read your piece and look at the chart.

Do you need to do any of these things? If there is something you can do, put your thumb up in the air! Wow, writers! It seems like you all have a lot to do. Keep going. And when you feel like you are done, check in with this chart again! I will hang it up here so you can see it and use it from your writing spot."

I also reminded them to visit the writing center if they needed more paper. I wanted them to become more independent at getting their own supplies when they needed them.

As Students Continue Working . . .

"Say the sounds slowly. Listen to the sounds and think, 'What letter makes that sound?'"

"Get a really clear picture of what you are making. Think about the size of it and the shape of it. And draw it the best you can!"

"Don't forget about our writing center, which has more paper when your caddy runs out. It's good to get to know how to go to the writing center, because we won't have paper at our tables for much longer. Soon we'll be getting our paper from the writing center all the time!"

"Don't be afraid of a hard idea! Be brave and go for it!"

continuum to pinpoint some of the areas that especially need to be addressed. At these early stages in your children's writing development, it is common that they might need some assistance in topic choice. Are they choosing topics that they know well and that are important to them? And are they communicating what they know through their pictures and words? Use your conferences and strategy groups to help address these common kindergarten hiccups.

Another of your goals will be to help children handle the rough spots that inevitably come as they learn to work in close quarters, so that the class becomes a collaborative community. With your guidance, children will come to value both supporting *and* learning from others. Children might complain, "You stole my idea!" Or "I'm going to tell on you." When problems like this arise, it is important to study them. Why might a writer be patterning her work entirely after the work of a classmate? Does she lack confidence in the importance of her own ideas? Does she need strategies for generating her own topic? Why might a writer be disturbing his tablemates? Has he forgotten the menu of ways to stay productive in writing workshop? Does the chart have words but no pictures to support him? It's wise to assume that your youngsters want to write and to do it well. If this is not happening, try to determine what is getting in the way so you can address it.

In the early part of kindergarten we must ensure that all children trust that they can be successful at the work we are asking them to do. Many youngsters walk into our classrooms believing that they don't yet know how to read or write. And of course most of them don't know how to decode or encode text, nor should they. When we invite them to share what they know, tell stories, and otherwise create meaning on paper, we tell them that this is what writing is all about—and it is! Composing ideas and making decisions about how to communicate them is at the heart of writing and is a more nuanced and complex process than encoding those ideas as print. And yet, some children will look at their work and say, "This isn't *real* writing." They will view their own attempts as failures to capture with perfection the ideas they'd hoped to represent. We know that a vital condition for learning is approximation—taking risks and learning from our attempts.

Our job as teachers, then, is to help children become more comfortable with, and even proud of, their approximations. One way this may manifest itself is in conferences with children who stare at their blank papers, afraid to make any marks at all, lest it be wrong or not good enough. In these conferences your teaching focus will probably not be on a writing skill, but rather on the very act of taking a risk. You might say, "Let me show you how I get myself started, even when I think I don't know how to do something, or even when I think I'll make a mistake. Let me show you how I bravely try." The other most common way you will need to address children's fear of approximation is in conferences with children who write the same few things over and over because these are the only things they think they know how to do. Again, your teaching focus here will probably not be a writing skill. Rather, you'll want to teach them how to cast a wider net for topics, taking a leap of faith in their own ability to say what they need to say on paper. You might say, "Today I was going to write about my mom and how I love her. I have gotten really good at that, and I know how to make all those words. But then I found five pieces in my folder that already say, 'I love Mom.' I realized I have so many other important things to write about, like dogs and recess and soccer and making cupcakes and the different things I know how to build with blocks! When you're five, you know a lot of important stuff! Of course, five-year-olds don't know all those words yet, but that doesn't mean they shouldn't be sharing their knowledge! When I realized that, I decided to write about something new today. Let me help you make a decision to write about something important to *you* today."

Sharing Strategies

Spotlight a child who has found a way to create a hard-to-draw picture.

Nicky stood beside me at the front of the meeting area. I had worked with him to press on in the face of difficulty and was now inviting him to share his success with the class (see Figure 6–1). "Well, um . . . I'm not done yet. But, I was trying to draw the ball going into the hoop cause my book's about playing the basketball games at the circus. It was easy to make the ball and the hoop. But some miss the first time."

"Yes, the ball and the hoop. They are here," I pointed to the picture. "So which part was tricky for you?" I looked back at his picture with a serious, inquisitive look on my face.

"The ball going into the hoop. I didn't know how to draw that." He paused and looked at me for reassurance.

"Go ahead, Nicky. What did you do next?"

"Well, I just remembered how you said to do the best we can, so I just put little arrows after the ball to show it was going down in the hoop."

"Hold it up for everyone to see, Nicky." He did and I pointed to what he did. "Nicky did the best he could, and he came up with a neat symbol to show that something is heading in a particular direction: arrows. Wow! A new way for us to show how something moves! It makes me think I could add an arrow to show the bees moving from flower to flower in my garden book!"

Recruit children to help you try the strategy in your shared piece.

I took out our playground book and started to look it over. "Are you thinking what I am thinking? Could we try Nicky's strategy here too? Where could we teach people about how we move on the playground? Turn and talk!" I gave them a minute and then called them back together.

Remind children that they can try the work of this session tomorrow and ever after, sharing ideas as they do so.

"Not just today, but whenever you come across a hard thing to draw or write, you can do what Nicky did. Do the best you can! And we can keep sharing cool ideas of how we do those things just like Nicky shared his trick about using an arrow! Writers don't give up, and writers learn from one another."

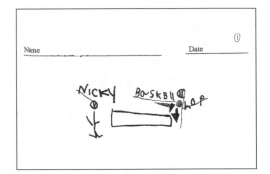
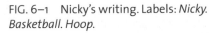

FIG. 6–1   Nicky's writing. Labels: *Nicky. Basketball. Hoop.*

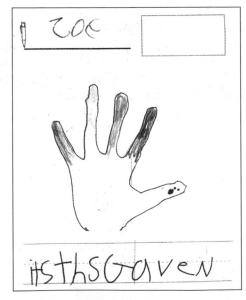

FIG. 6–2   Another example—Zoe's writing. *It's Thanksgiving.* She uses her fingers to show a hard-to-draw turkey.

Turning Pieces into Scrolls and Books

IN THIS SESSION, you'll teach students that when writers want to teach more, they add more pages to their book.

GETTING READY

✔ Partnership chart and masking tape on the rug to assign seats (see Connection)

✔ *Farm Animals* (DK Readers pre-Level 1) and other teaching books or other texts to model with (see Connection and Active Engagement)

✔ A student's piece of writing to use as a model, with additional pages ready to attach to make a booklet (see Teaching)

✔ Your own demonstration text from the day before, with additional pages ready to tape together to make a scroll (see Teaching)

✔ The class's shared playground piece (see Active Engagement)

✔ Writing folders

✔ Tape and mini-staplers (see Teaching, Active Engagement, and Link)

✔ Several photographs of flowers with one photo that does not belong in the group (see Share)

✔ "I Can Revise My Teaching Book" chart (see Share)

TODAY is one of the most exciting days in the entire year. Bring out the streamers, the fireworks! Expect that your children's growth, after today, will accelerate at a great clip. Today begins the second bend in the road of the unit. This upcoming bend is devoted to the principle that writers add on not just by cramming more pictures and words onto singe sheets of paper. Writers also staple and tape, and in doing so, they turn "pieces" into books and reports.

The bend will begin with you teaching writers to tape more paper onto the bottoms of their writing or to staple more pages behind their first page, letting their work become as long as Chinese dragons or as thick as *Freight Train*. Materials carry messages. As you provision your students with tape and staplers, you're conveying an important message: writers write not just pages, not just pieces, but *books*!

As the bend progresses, you'll move from teaching children that they can add on in these ways to providing them with support for this large-scale revision work. That support will come in the form of a long-term writing partner. Children can learn to read their writing with a partner, using their partners' responses to lead toward additional revision. Most state standards call for kindergarten writers and readers to seek help and get more information from each other to clarify information. We want to reinforce all of these things in our writing workshop. Not only does it improve children's speaking and listening skills to work with a partner in these ways, but it also helps them live their identities as writers. They'll also need to learn the reciprocal side of this. That is, they need to learn to become good partners for each other, listening to each other in ways that help writers want to say more.

Once children are writing teaching books, it will be quite a natural thing for you to teach them that they actually do not need to write and then add on, little by little. Instead, they can plan on writing longer books from the start, and to do this, it helps to use partners to support not just adding on, but also planning.

Turning Pieces into Scrolls and Books

CONNECTION

Orchestrate children sitting in long-term partnerships, talking up these relationships as support for the breakthrough work children will do in the upcoming portion of the unit.

Before convening children, I had determined partnerships and placed masking tape labeled with kids' names on the rug to indicate where each duo would sit. I took care that children needing special attention were at the front.

"Writers, when I call you to come to the meeting area, you'll need to find your name on a piece of tape on the rug and sit there." Once children had gathered, I said, "Writers, today we are going to begin a whole new chapter in our writing workshop. Starting today, you won't just be writing pages—you'll be writing a whole lot more. This is a big deal, so I need to tell you a secret about writing books. Listen closely." I leaned toward the class, and whispered, "This book *says* that it was written by Donald Crews, but *really*, he had a helper! He got ideas from a helper! Almost nobody writes a book without a helper. So today, because we are going to start doing work that is a lot harder and longer, I want to first give each one of you a helper. You'll see on this chart that I have given each of you a writing partner, a writing helper. When you read your name, will you and your new writing partner shake hands?" Children did this, and then I started the rest of the minilesson.

Tell children about a writer who was squeezing more onto a page than was reasonable, using this as a prelude to teaching children that professional writers add on more pages.

"The other day Mikey was scrunched over his writing, like this." I made my body into a ball, elbow jutted out. "He was so close to his paper it looked like he might go cross-eyed! I peered over his shoulder to see what he was doing, and guess what I saw? In the corner of his paper was a teeny tiny drawing that Mikey was struggling to make. When I asked him why he was going to all that trouble, he said he'd forgotten to put his hamster's drinking water and there was no more room on the page.

◆ COACHING

In your classroom, you will want to decide how to gather students, how to get students to turn and talk with one another, and how to pace your lessons so that you have enough workshop time to get to writing. Developing rug spots for (or with) your students is a helpful management tool, so that each day students know where to sit and whom to talk to. This will save time going forward.

You are also beginning to introduce the concept of partnerships. Here in the meeting area, each student will have a partner to work with, someone with whom to share thoughts, ideas, and writing. In this connection you will see how I invoke Donald Crews, our mentor author for this part of the unit. I want students to start seeing themselves as writers with writer's needs—in this instance, to have partners and make booklets.

"Well, that got me thinking that not just Mikey but *all of you* might need to do something that professional writers do all the time! Can you guess what that is?" The kids looked confused.

"Remember this book on animals that live on the farm that I showed you our first day together?" I held it up for them to see. "Look. On the first page is a . . . and on the next page is . . . and on the third page . . . . Are you noticing what I'm noticing? There is *more than one page*! In fact, there are more than fifteen pages! And each page teaches a different thing."

❧ **Name the teaching point.**

"Today I want to teach you that when writers want to teach more, they add more pages to their books. We can use either a stapler to turn pages into a book, or tape to turn pages into what people call a scroll."

TEACHING

Recruit the class to help one child turn a page of writing into a book.

"So let's see if we can help Mikey with his book about hamsters. Mikey, will you bring me what you have so far?" When Mikey was standing by my side, I held up his page for the class to see. "Ah, here's your hamster in its wheel. What a nice big picture this is. It looks like the hamster is running. Is that right, Mikey?" Mikey nodded. "So one thing you're teaching us is that hamsters run on wheels. Great. Now, let's see." I examined the page and said, "Mikey, is this your hamster's water feeder, here in the corner?" Again, Mikey nodded. "Well, that teaches me that hamsters don't drink out of cups like people, or out of dishes like cats and dogs. They drink out of what looks like a straw."

"It's a water bottle," Mikey offered.

"Oh, I see. Yes, there's this little tube attached to a larger bottle of water. And I'm guessing that the hamster sips water through the tube. That's so neat!

"Mikey, you are definitely ready to add pages to this piece. Besides running out of room on your page, you have more than just one thing to teach. Page one teaches us that hamsters run on wheels. And page two can teach that hamsters drink out of tubes attached to a water bottle. I bet you have something else you could teach about hamsters. Am I right?"

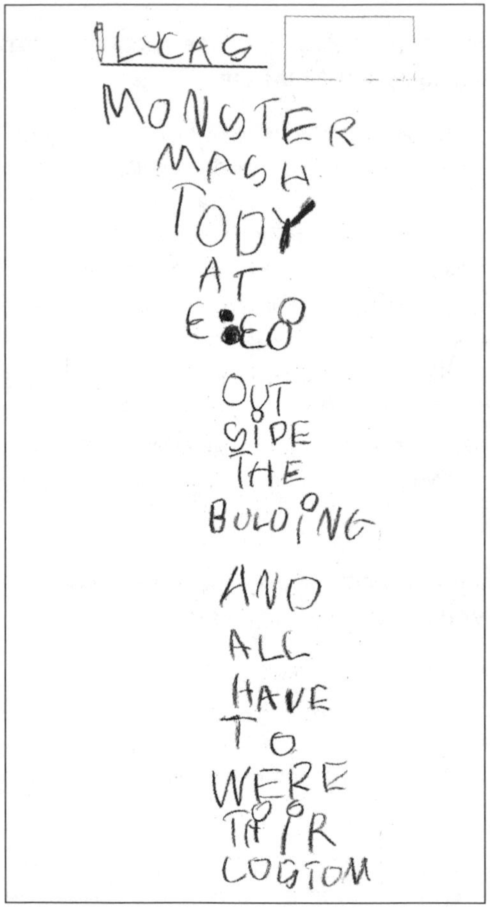

In this lesson, I decide to use a piece of student writing to help exemplify the teaching point. Demonstrating with a variety of texts is a powerful way, in a unit of study, to capture students' attention. When students see their peers' work up on the board in front of them, oftentimes this ignites an excitement and newfound attention to learning. I make a big deal about how much Mikey's piece teaches. I want the other students to see the amount of information that Mikey is teaching, before I suggest making a booklet.

FIG. 7–1   Lucas's scroll: *Monster Mash today at 8:00 outside the building and all have to wear their costume.*

You have to have fun.

Mikey nodded and said, "Yeah, like about what they eat. Also about their toys, and how you clean their cage."

Demonstrate stapling pages together to make a book for one child, suggesting others can do similar work.

"Oh my goodness, Mikey! This is a big day. You're ready to be an author like the authors in our library. You're ready to add pages to your piece so that you can teach more than one thing. It's time to make a booklet!"

I picked up a few blank pages and laid them behind Mikey's single page about his hamster. Then I placed the pages into the stapler and demonstrated how to staple the pages. I stapled the top and middle staples and then asked Mikey to staple the bottom." Then I picked up the book, leafed through its pages, handed it ceremoniously to Mikey, and said, "Your very first book! I bet we could all make books!"

Demonstrate taping pages together to make a scroll with your own writing, suggesting others can do similar work.

"Let me show you another way we can add to our work. This is my gymnastics book from yesterday. I worked really hard on it, and I couldn't fit all of my ideas onto one page. I *could* make a book, just like Mikey did, but watch what else I can make. Lean in close because this is really, really cool. I can tape the second page to the bottom of the first page like this." I taped the pages together and held it up for all to see. Then I added another page and held it up again. A couple of children gasped. "I know! It's getting so long! Look at how much I wrote! Are you wondering how I'm going to put it away, since I don't have a folder that's as tall as Sebastian? I roll it up like this." I started rolling the scroll. "And now it's nice and small. This can go into my folder. Neat, huh? We can all start to make books and scrolls today, Super Writers! We can add pages and staple or tape them together to make books *and* scrolls about your topics!"

ACTIVE ENGAGEMENT

Recruit children to join you in studying a nonfiction text to infer the logic behind the organizational structure.

"Writers, I have a bunch of books from our library up here on the easel. They are all teaching books. Let's study them together and notice what the authors did. Here is the first: It is called *Farm Animals*. Let's read what this author taught us on this first page":

> Come meet my friends at the farm.

"And look, we can learn a lot about the organizational structure from this page in *Farm Animals*. We can read the labels: *farmhouse* and *barn*. But wait. What's this? What comes next? *Another page!* This tells about a farm animal living on this farm. What do you think will come on the next page?"

Children called out other farm animals. "It makes so much sense for you to guess that in this book, the pages will all tell about different farm animals. Let's see what's next." We turned the pages ahead and noted a page on a turkey and another on ducks and ducklings. "Do you think there will be a page about cooking brownies in this book?"

You will notice that here in the teaching I do two quick demonstration. After I demonstrate with Mikey's piece, I turn to my own writing, in which I talk about how I, too, can add on, or can make a scroll. I am trying to show students that they have options; that there isn't just one way to make their books. I want to be sure that I am constantly opening the doors to creativity and inventiveness rather than confining students' ingenuity to a one-way approach to writing.

This is a variation of the active engagement part of a minilesson. You will notice that I get the students to engage with thinking about how the pages of a book fit together. This is to support them with the understanding of why books need pages and how books work. It serves as a wonderful reading-writing connection, not only because it is a book that many of them can learn how to read, but also because it is teaching them about the text structures in a book and how we can use that knowledge to help us make predictions, learn new information, and get ready to read the words on the page.

"Noooo!" the children chorused.

"That's right, because it is all about animals that live on a farm. Each page has a different thing about farm animals. It teaches us about the babies, where they live, and even what some of their body parts are called."

Turn to the class book and recruit children to suggest ways to extend that book.

I took out the class book. "Now let's look at our book about the playground. Uh-oh. Wait, it's not a book! It doesn't have another page! It's not a scroll, either! Oh no! What should we do? Quickly, with your writing partner, turn and talk about what we should do with our playground piece."

The children talked.

"Great suggestions, everyone. You are right that I can take out the stapler or tape and add another page or two to make it a book or a scroll, and then we could put pages that show other places where we play."

LINK

Send children off to turn their pages into books and scrolls.

"Writers, today is a special day because we are ready to turn our pages into books and scrolls! When you finish one page you can think about what else you have to teach about your topic, and you can add on pages if you need to! That is not just true today, that is true forever! You will have to decide, 'Will I tape my pages, or will I staple my pages together?' I have tape and mini-staplers in your caddies for you to use! If you need more paper, you can go to the writing center and get more paper if your caddie runs out.

"You have so many ways you can work today, don't you?" I gestured toward our chart. "Go ahead, now, and write!"

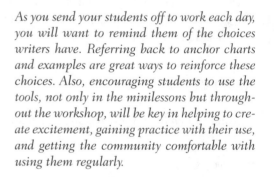

As you send your students off to work each day, you will want to remind them of the choices writers have. Referring back to anchor charts and examples are great ways to reinforce these choices. Also, encouraging students to use the tools, not only in the minilessons but throughout the workshop, will be key in helping to create excitement, gaining practice with their use, and getting the community comfortable with using them regularly.

When We Are Done, We Have Just Begun

We can:

- add to our pictures
- add to our words
- start a new piece
- reread our writing

Encouraging Children to Add to Their Work While Nurturing Confidence and Building Enthusiasm

ONCE DON GRAVES, a great leader in the field of writing, began a speech about teaching writing by asking a roomful of teachers to list their children and then, alongside each child's name, to write about what that child knows. Beside one child's name, for example, a teacher might have written, "Emma is an expert on playing with Legos, having a baby brother, and sharing a bedroom." Don explained that the teaching of writing begins with knowing our students' areas of expertise and letting them teach us what they know. The writing workshop gives you a wonderful chance to find out what your students know. Especially at the start of the year, you need to listen hard. Let each child make you laugh, wince, or gasp. Your big-eyed attentiveness matters, and your questions matter. Be prepared to extend what children say to you. Once a child teaches you his or her content, you'll want to say, "Wow, I see part of that on your paper, but you told me some things that are not yet on your paper. You know even more than you already wrote! You need to add another page!"

In a way, this is Day One of the writing workshop all over again. you will once again be issuing a generous invitation to children, inviting them to role-play their way into being the writers you hope they become. As with Day One, you have to foster a sense of "I can do this! I really can!" So it will be more important to highlight their successes than to point out their areas of need. Your conferences will focus on all kinds of approximations. Try not to think of them as mess-ups, even though they might look that way. A child will have a book entitled, "My Dad," containing an equal number of pages about the sports team or school or any other topic that came to the child's mind. Another child might put the same exact floating figure on every page, just to fill a book. Yet another might be suddenly paralyzed by the challenge of adding pages and write nothing at all. Some will not know how to elaborate and so will add to their writing by repeating what they have already written. And, of course, many others will take to the challenge like fish to water.

The important thing for today is that you rally heaps and heaps of resolve and ambition in your youngsters. Children are dying to write books and will work morning, noon, and night to do so. So use today's minilesson and the invitation you are offering to tap into a great energy source in children, and use that energy to help children grow. One way to do this is to carry a couple of favorite published books from your classroom library

around with you as you confer. Say to children, "Let's study what this author did in his writing because yours may be somewhat similar." Or "You could make a cover and an 'about the author' page for your book, just like this author did!" What is essential is that you tap the excitement of today's work and use it to support children's progress.

Try not to worry that children in your classroom are not up to the task or not ready yet to make books. Imagine if we didn't engage babies in conversations until they could correctly pronounce whole sentences. If we don't engage youngsters in the real work of writing books until they can accurately write whole sentences, we risk slowing their learning. Anything you've learned to do probably required some effort, some hard work, but you were glad to do it because the work felt consequential to you. So yes, you will still want to remind children to write as well as to draw, and remind them of everything else they have learned so far. But the teaching that will matter most will involve helping children see that they are the kind of writers who make books! They are the kind of writers who fill pages! They are the kind of writers who have more to say and know how to say it!

MID-WORKSHOP TEACHING **Making Cover Pages with Titles**

"Writers, check to make sure that all your pages really go together! Daniel did. He read each page of his book and then thought, 'Yep, all these pages are about different characters in *Star Wars!*' So he made a cover and then he even gave his book a title—'A Book about Star Wars!' Reread your books right now, and make sure that all the pages you stapled together are about the same topic. If they are, then you can make a cover and title if you want, just like Daniel did! If not, fix your book so that all the pages *do* go together! You might need to take the pages apart so you can take out any that don't go with the rest. Maybe you'll use those pages for another book, so don't throw them away."

(continues)

"Emma is stapling on another page to add information!"

"Deja realized she doesn't have any more space to add information about her dog, just like Mikey. So she got more pages to add her information *across* pages (see Figure 7–2). When you're done, reread and think to yourself, 'Can I add more pictures? More words? Or another page?' Think about all three things."

"Kevin did something so smart. He wrote a book about SpongeBob," I showed one page, "and then he realized he needed another page to show the other characters in the television show! So he got another page from the writing center and he stapled it, just like this."

FIG. 7–2 Deja's writing: *I have a dog. Get food. Drinks water. The dogs bark at each other.* (Labels: *Drink. Bark. Get food. Eat.*)

The dogs eat. I play with the dog in my house. (Labels: *Me. Play. Brother. Door.*)

Dogs play with each other. (Labels: *Dogs. Play.*)

Dogs fight with each other. This is the cage. (Labels: *Fight. Cage.*)

Making Sure All the Pages in Your Book Go Together

Recruit students to work together to determine whether their books are about one topic or more.

"Writers, quiet as mice, please come to the meeting area and sit next to your writing partner. If you forgot where to go, look for your name on the floor. You are going to work with your partner to think about the books that you are writing. When writers revise, sometimes they add pages to their books or scrolls. Sometimes they take out parts that don't belong. The two of you will work together to figure out whether the book you each wrote and stapled together is really *one* book or whether one or both of you accidentally put together *more than one* book when you started to staple!

"Writers, to give you a little practice, first I am going to show you some photographs. It's your job to tell me if they all go with the topic, flowers. As I show you each photograph, put your thumb on your knee if you think it could go in a book called *Flowers*. If it doesn't, wave your hand like this." I demonstrated a "no-go" hand wave.

"Here is a field of sunflowers." I paused and looked for a thumb or a wave of the hand. "I see lots of thumbs on knees. Yep, sunflowers are flowers. What about a vase of roses? Yep. It also goes with flowers. What about an apple blossom? Yep, it does. Even though it grows on a tree, it's still a flower. What about this pond? Wait, is this a flower? Does this photo teach us about flowers?" The children made the "no-go" wave with their hands. "Nope! You are right. This photo needs to come out because it is teaching about a pond, *not* a flower!

"We're going to take turns being readers and listeners, so quickly decide which of you will be the reader first. Now, hold the book between you. Ready? Readers, read your pages. Listeners, as your partner reads, think about whether the pages belong together or whether your partner accidentally mixed in pages that should go into a different book." After a bit, I signaled to the children to switch roles so that each child got a turn to be both reader and listener.

Celebrate writers who found two (or more) books in one.

"Everybody listen to what Owen did. His book is about animals that live in the ocean. When he was reading, he and his partner noticed a page about tigers! Owen loves tigers, but they don't live in the ocean. He was about to think he had made a big mistake, and he was even getting a little sad, but then he realized he could start a *whole new book* with the tiger page! Isn't that amazing? What? That happened to you, too, Matthew? Thank goodness we have partners!"

If you need to, you can use the share to remind writers to treat their work with care. You might say something like, "So as you go back to your seats to put your writing away, be sure to put your books into your folders carefully. I was looking at your writing last weekend, and I saw that some of you had jammed your writing into your folder like this," I demonstrated shoving a piece of paper into a folder, "and it was all scrunched up! How sad! That's not how writers treat their writing. They use their hands to straighten out all their pieces of writing into a neat pack and then slide them into the pocket." I demonstrated neatening up a pile of papers and sliding it nicely into a folder pocket. "Let's try to take better care of our precious amazing writing—especially now that we're making books!"

"I am going to start a new chart, titled 'I Can Revise My Teaching Book.'

"I am going to have some examples of your work next to these points so we remember to do them."

FIG 7–3   Paloma's writing: *This is our school. School is exciting. School is kind. School is for everyone.* Notice how, with each big idea, she starts a new page.

Planning Teaching Books Page by Page

S OMETIMES WHEN YOU ARE TEACHING youngsters to do things like stapling or touching pages and saying aloud what they will write, it is possible to think of the work as child's play, not recognizing that in fact the work you are supporting undergirds a great deal of writing development. Today your teaching is informed by the fact that you are teaching students to write informational texts. They may only be five years old, and their texts are a far cry from the research reports these children will produce a decade from now, but this lesson invites kids to approximate some of the moves that informational writers make. You are teaching elaboration, and for the next ten years, this will be something that students continue to study. You are also teaching students to approach the challenge of writing informational texts, aware from the start that planning is important. For now, of course, your emphasis on organization is lightly done. But when you tell children that on each page, they write something different about their topic, you are gesturing toward the more extensive planning work students will be doing soon.

Your instruction is not just informed by the knowledge of how children develop as informational writers, you are also teaching students about the writing process. As youngsters grow, their writing process options grow richer, their repertoire of skills grows greater. So, early in this unit, children rehearsed by thinking of their topic, picturing it, and then putting it on the page. Now, they are rehearsing by thinking about all they know about their topic, dividing that information up so that chunks go on different pages, and then, again, envisioning and writing. You have also added another step. Writers don't just see in their mind's eye what they will write. They also say it, hearing their words before they capture them on the page.

Your teaching needs always to be informed not just by a sense of the trajectory of development you are supporting, but also by a sense of the plot line of the unit. This bend in the road of this unit is a short one. You'll continue to support students in writing information books for a few days, and then you'll let students know that they will be publishing the best of their books. Then, instruction will turn toward preparing a text for a reader.

IN THIS SESSION, you'll teach students that when writers write a whole book, they plan how that book will go.

GETTING READY

✔ Partnership chart (see Connection)

✔ Prestapled booklets, one per partnership (see Connection)

✔ A student's piece of writing to use for demonstration (see Connection)

✔ Student writing folders (see Share)

✔ Your own writing folder, with unfinished writing for you to come back to (see Share)

✔ Post-it notes (see Share)

Planning Teaching Books Page by Page

CONNECTION

Introduce the new designation of some partners as 1 and others as 2.

"Writers, I want to show you something before you come to the meeting area today. Take a look at our partnership chart, and you will see 1 above some names and 2 above the others. From now on, some of you will be 1 partners, and some will be 2. This way when we turn and talk, or do other things, it will be easy to figure out who goes first. As you come over to the meeting area, you are going to see that I have put booklets on all the 1 rug spots. Will 1 partners please come over and sit on the little booklets? We will be working with them in our lesson today. Okay, now all Partner 2s come to the meeting area. Don't worry about not having booklets. You are actually going to share the booklets, but only Partners 1 gets to sit on them today."

Acknowledge children's success in adding to their writing.

"Super Writers, I was looking at Liam's writing, and two days ago, his writing looked like this." I held up a page. "*Now* his writing looks like this." I held up a scroll. "It is almost as tall as Liam. Did anyone have your writing go from being little to being big—overnight—like Liam did?" Many children signaled that they had.

"How many of you wrote a book yesterday?" I noted the thumbs up. "How many of you wrote a scroll like Liam did yesterday?" Again, I noted the thumbs up.

"This is amazing. Kids are *supposed* to grow bit by bit, inch by inch. Your writing grew from here," I touched my knee, "to here," I reached way up in the air on my tip-toes, "in one day. And it grew like that because you learned that you can add on and on and on and *on*!"

"The cool thing is that you didn't just make books and scrolls yesterday. You made *yourselves* into new kinds of writers, because from this day forward, for the rest of your life, you can now be the kind of writer who writes not just pieces, not just pages, but *books*."

◆ COACHING

Be sure that at this point in the unit your writing center contains some prestapled booklets and some single sheets. You will also want to have some paper with a big box and one line and some paper with a big box and two or three lines. Because your writers are growing, you want to be sure the paper and the lines match with where they are developmentally. When you see that children are using many letters and sounds in their labels, this is a sign that they are ready for sentences. If you have students who were writing a sentence or two at the beginning of the unit, many are probably ready to write more by now. Providing paper that invites students to "write" more helps students push themselves to add more words on the page. Ask yourself, "Am I getting a lot of writing? Could this student do more if she had more lines?"

❖ Name the teaching point.

"Today I want to teach you that writers of books take time to plan how their pages will go. Writers don't just write one page and then say, 'Oops. I want to add another.' Instead, writers know from the start that they will be writing a whole book, and they plan out how that whole book will go."

TEACHING AND ACTIVE ENGAGEMENT

Let students know that today you are going to teach by coaching them, rather than by demonstrating for them.

"In today's minilesson, I'm not going to do this work and then tell you what I did and then say, 'Now you try it.' Instead, how about if you all are the first ones to do this? I'll see if I can coach you, and *you do it*, not me."

Support students in coming up with topics for teaching books, since they will need these to go ahead with the rest of the lesson.

"The first thing we need to do is come up with topics for teaching books. I'll give you both a minute to think and talk together. What is something that you know and care about? If one of you is having trouble thinking of a topic, that's a great thing for your partner to help with. Show me a thumb when you both have topics ready. Ooh, Margay, that was so fast! Wow! Okay, now I see a bunch of thumbs. Great! We're ready to plan how our books could go."

Coach partners to touch the pages of their booklets, talking about what they might write on each one.

"Partner 1, take out the booklet and hold it with Partner 2. Look at the cover. That probably will have something about your topic on it, right? Now open the book. Touch the first page and tell your partner what you might draw and write on it. When you're ready, turn the page! Yes, just like that! Keep going. Touch each page in your booklet and talk about the information you could draw and write. Don't forget to *turn the page!*"

As children worked in partnerships, I coached.

"Turn the page!"

"What else could you teach?"

"Touch each page and say what you are going to teach on that page."

When they'd had a minute or two to work on this, I stopped them to highlight an example from the class. "Writers, listen to what Margay said about writing a teaching book about songs." I held her book open to the first page and said, "On this page she said she could write stars for 'Twinkle Twinkle Little Star.' Then she *turned the page!*" I said, making a grand gesture of turning the page. "On this page she said she could write about the itsy-bitsy spider being caught in the rain. And then she *turned the page.*" I flipped to the next page. "And on this page she thought she might write

You will want to be sure that you do two things in the workshop. First, honor and follow what kids can do, finding ways to help them think about the best ways to plan, write, and elaborate in their writing. Second, nudge them and invite them to try and use new strategies as well. That is exactly what I am doing here, trying to ratchet up students' understanding about what it means to write by showing them a new, more sophisticated way to plan. This lesson is intentionally designed without a demonstration so that your students get a lot of practice, not only in manipulating a booklet, but also in rehearsing and telling their information. This oral language rehearsal helps kids clarify and think about what they are going to write and often helps them generate more content. Manipulating the booklet simultaneously helps kids to think about how the book will actually go and also how they will place their information across the pages. Some students will realize they need more pages. Some will forget to turn the page. Others will not know what to do with the extra page because they have "run out" of things to teach. All of these scenarios will come true. And this is one of the main reasons why writers plan!

about 'Mary Had a Little Lamb.' Wow! Partner 2, now it's your turn to plan a teaching book. Partner 1, hand over the booklet! Partner 2, do you remember what *your* teaching book could be about? Now touch each page and tell your partner what you could write. Go!"

After the partners had worked together for a minute or two, I called them back together to share what one child had done. "Writers, stop, look, and listen."

"Yeah!" The children sang back.

LINK

Send them off, reminding them of the importance of planning before they write.

"Casey did a really important thing that writers do. She said, 'I only have three pages here, but I need more because I want to write about all the cool tricks you can do in soccer, and I know way more than three! I need more pages.' Did you hear how Casey thought about what she wanted to write before she even picked up a pencil? She made a plan, and her plan told her how many pages she would need!

"You are all really starting to get the idea of how writers plan! We talk about our ideas for each page and we get what we need. We may even realize, like Casey did, that we need more pages! So as you start new pieces, you can do this, too. You can stop and ask yourself, 'What are all the things I need to teach people about my topic?' You can touch each page and, as you do so, think about the information that you might draw and write on that page. And you do this planning from now on through the rest of your life, not just today. Writers plan!"

"Partner 1, if you are starting a new piece of writing today, take the booklet and go get started. If you are not, give it to Partner 2. Now Partner 2, if you are going to start a new piece, take that booklet and get started. Remember to plan what you are going to write by touching each page and thinking about what you will write on each one. If you need more paper, get more paper from the writing center.

"Everyone who's *not* starting a new piece today, you can go back to your writing spots and work on books or scrolls in your folder. Off you go. Now the rest of you."

Coaching Students to Return to Unfinished Work

YOUR WORKSHOP will have been underway for a week or two now, so this is a good time to pause and reflect on what your children have learned. Reread your goals for the unit and consider your children's progress toward obtaining those goals. It will be important to notice whether your children have developed strategies for writing teaching texts. You want them to approach writing brimming with content and eager to use any means possible to convey that content. As you add new conferences to your repertoire, don't forget the ones you learned early on. Remember especially the early emphasis on listening attentively to the child's meaning.

Many kindergarten teachers look for opportunities to link the work that they do in writing workshop with other parts of the day. For instance, you may notice children making plans for how to build an airport in the block center during choice time (or work time, as some teachers call it). Others may step back from their easels to look at the whole painting to see what they need to add. You might hear a child excitedly call to his friend, "Come look at my space tractor!" These are opportunities to point out that they are doing exactly what writers do. "Wow! You are someone who plans before you build (or adds to your work or shares your work with friends). That must be so helpful when you write!"

You might even share some particularly interesting observations with the rest of the class during a minilesson. "Writers, I was so excited yesterday. During choice time, Tanisa and Hailey were making a barn, and first they made it in a quick fashion—just a square for horses. But then they looked at it and said, 'Wait! We should have a place for the saddles and the hay—a place where the horses can't go!' They added that. Then they got the idea to make different stalls for different horses. But the sad thing was it was time for lunch. Listen to what they did next. They got the idea to put a green dot on a paper and leave it here beside their barn as a 'still-working-on-this' message to the rest of us. And today during choice time they went back to their barn. I know that yesterday, at the end of writing time, some of you did the same thing. You put your writing in the still-working-on-it section. Thumbs up if you did that! Let's have you start with that piece today. Instead of starting a new piece, remember what you wrote and tell your partners what else you can imagine adding today, right now! Tell the person next to you. It'll be just like what Tanisa and Hailey did." Making connections like these helps children see that writing is not a separate new thing but an extension of what they already do in their talk and in their play.

You may have noticed a small group of students who tend to write a page, or even an entire booklet, but by the end forget what they have written. You'll want to teach

---

MID-WORKSHOP TEACHING
Using a Newly Established Writing Partner Meeting Area

"Writers, Daniel just asked me if it would be okay to talk out the plan for his teaching book with his partner before he writes it. I said, 'Yes, absolutely, what a spectacular idea!' See this table, over here, by the window, with two chairs? This will be a place for partners to meet if they want to read their writing to each other or talk over their writing plans. After you meet, head back to your writing spots so you can get right back to your writing. If someone is already here, though, you'll have to use your two-inch voice and wait your turn! Now back to work, Super Writers."

As Students Continue Working . . .

"If you need more paper, don't forget to staple and add on."

"Fill up each page with lots of details."

"Don't forget to add your words on *all* your pages."

"When you start a new piece, get a booklet! Think about how many pages you might need!"

them some strategies to help them remember what their writing was about. Teach them that three things are really helpful for reminding us what our writing says: drawing specific information about a topic, writing words and labels, and rereading it many times along the way. As the students get started on their writing, begin coaching each child. Remind students to reread their work often and encourage them to add more to the drawing or to the words and labels. Help them think of information that will help them remember what the page says. You may also decide for yourself to write the words down, possibly on a Post-it, so that when you come back around to coach the same child you'll know if their words are similar to what they said before. Also, if they get terribly stuck, you can refer to these notes to jog their memory. After being part of a small group to work on naming, drawing, and writing, Aleysha was able to write a teaching book about fish. Notice how Aleysha is not only able to organize her writing and give information, but with scaffolding and support she also gets her words written. She started this work in the small group and was then able to carry on with the other pages on her own (see Figure 8–1).

Remember that if you introduce a new special tool or structure for writers to use, such as a partner meeting table, everyone will want to use it for a few days. Some children will go to the table just for the sake of trying out the new thing, rather than to meet purposefully with a partner. Don't worry if there's a big initial run on the table. It will soon become another familiar element of writing workshop, and children will learn to use it well, just as they did with the date stamps.

FIG. 8–1   Aleysha's writing: *Fish swim in water.*   *My cousin has a fish. She grabs the fish. She*   *Fish eat food.* (Label: *Food.*)
(Label: *Fish. Swim.*)   *play with the fish.* (Labels: *Cousin. Fish. Cage.*)

Going Back to Old Pieces and Writing More

Show children that they can add on to pieces they thought were finished.

"Writers, some of you have been saying it is hard to think about something new to teach others. Remember that red dot side of your folder? You've each got lots of finished pieces on that side. I know you made the decision that those pieces were finished, but here's the thing. Sometimes writers reread old, finished pieces and realize, 'Hey, there's something good here that I could make into a longer piece. This little finished page deserves to be a book!' Then they take that little bit of writing, that start of an idea, and they grow it into something much bigger.

"Earlier today, I decided to peek inside my own folder on the red dot side. Look what I found! Here is that piece about my grandmother's garden. Remember this one? I thought it was finished, so it put it on this side of my folder, but now that we've been working so hard to make books and scrolls, I'm realizing I have so much more to teach people about

FIG. 8–3 Zoey's writing. Labels: *Nuts. Owls.*
Zoey adds to her writing. Labels: *Birds. Sun. Pears.*
Zoey's writing. Labels: *Bananas. Squirrels. Tree. Bark.* Her pages are filling up!
Zoey's last page. Labels: *Owl. Night. Moon. Apples. The Trees.*

this topic. I went to the writing center and got some more paper, and now I'm going to plan how each page can go. Watch! I can add in the vegetable patch where she grows zucchinis! And I can add a page with her herb garden, where I pick fresh basil!

"Our writing folders are treasure chests of topics. So when you're not sure what your next teaching book might be, look in your folder first. You might find a great topic that you can add on to!

"Let's give it a try right now. Open your folder and read through your red dot side. Do you have a teaching page that you could turn into a book? When you find one, hold it up! Partner 2, can you share with Partner 1 what new pages you could add? Now Partner 1, you do the same.

"Tomorrow is a new day. I am going to give each of you a Post-it to put on top of the page of writing you chose. This way, when you open your folder tomorrow you'll remember that this is a piece you want to add on to. Move this piece of writing to the green dot side of your folder, and put it on top of the rest of the pieces on that side. Tomorrow will be another busy writing day!"

Asking and Answering Questions to Add More

ONE OF THE WONDERFUL THINGS about teaching children to write well is that learning to write strengthens their ability to read, and vice versa. We know that reading with the eyes of writers can take writers' work to new levels. The same is true when we challenge our writers with work that can actually lift the level of their independent reading. Planning writing lessons with an eye toward supporting reading work can help us bolster students' abilities in both areas.

Today's session is another opportunity to help your writers realize they have more to say, to convey to writers that revision matters and that writing means caring about making your work the best it can possibly be. It is an opportunity to get your writers to revise not only the draft on which they are currently working, but all of the booklets in their folders. Today's work supports stamina and drawing on a repertoire of strategies, and it is also an opportunity to support your writers in doing work that state standards require of them as *readers*.

Today you will teach your writers that they can work with partners to ask questions of each other's teaching texts and write and draw more to answer these questions. They will begin to learn to pay attention to the key details of their teaching texts and remind themselves to add these details to make their work stronger. And you will help writers see that the questions they ask of each other can become ones that they will soon ask of themselves as they internalize revision strategies. Then, in reading workshop, you can remind them of today's writing work, helping them to see that readers ask the same questions as writers do, and that the answers are the key details, the ones that matter most.

IN THIS SESSION, you'll teach students that writing partners help each other add more to their writing.

GETTING READY

- ✔ Chart paper and markers

- ✔ One page of your own sparse writing about an unusual object that students will have lots of questions about (this minilesson spotlights a honeycomb). Pick an object you can bring into the classroom so that students can examine it and ask questions.

- ✔ In-progress student writing (see Active Engagement)

- ✔ "I Can Revise My Teaching Book" chart (see Link)

- ✔ A child volunteer whom you and the class interview about his or her writing process. (see Share)

Asking and Answering Questions to Add More

CONNECTION

Remind children of the work they have been doing with partners.

"Writers, as you come to the meeting area, bring a piece of writing that you are working on, sit next to your partner, and sit on your writing. One, two, three, go!"

Once children had settled, I said, "Earlier I let you in on the secret that a book may have one author's name on the cover—like this one has Donald Crews's name—but that really, one author doesn't write a book all alone. Donald Crews had helpers. Almost every writer has helpers. And that is why you have partners.

"Yesterday, partners helped writers get ready to write their teaching books, planning writing across the pages of a booklet. And that is great because partners do help writers *before* a book is written."

Name the teaching point.

"Today I want to teach you that partners also help writers *after* a book is written, when the writer is thinking, 'I'm done.' Specifically, a partner reads a writer's book and then asks, 'What questions does this book give me?' And then the partner asks the writer questions. Those questions help the writer know what to add on."

TEACHING

Ask the class to be your writing partner and invite them to ask questions about your writing. Point out that "where," "how," and "why" questions help writers discover what they can add to their writing.

"Will you all be my writing partner, just to practice? And then you can be partners for each other. So, to be my partner, you need to ask me to read my writing to you, and then you need to listen really, really hard so you get what I said and so you can ask questions about parts I didn't explain. Is one of you going to get me started?"

I shifted into the role, and shaking out my hand, said, "I'm done. I finished my teaching book. I am putting it in my done folder now." I paused and then said, "So, everyone, what do you do to be good partners for me?"

Sometimes you'll sense that children are eager to get back to work. In those cases, cutting your talking to the bare bones can give them the time to write, write, write!

One of the children said, "Will you read us your writing?"

"Okay," I said. "I'd be happy to. It is about something I found on the way to school." Then I read a book that went like this.

> Today on the way to school I found a honeycomb.
> It looks really weird.
> It is a bee's house.

I also showed children my honeycomb, and when they were bustling with interest, saying things like, "What is it? That is weird! What is it for? Whoa!" I channeled their interest toward the work of being good partners." The children knew that partners ask questions, and they were keen to do so. Crawling on their knees, one child after another shot me questions. "Where did you find it?" asked Gabriela.

"I found it outside, right under a tree." I answered, and then pointed to Matthew.

"Why does it look weird?" Mathew asked.

"It has all these holes all over it. Holes are where bees put their honey and their babies," I answered.

Then I paused the class and said, "Your questions have gotten me thinking that I need to show and tell more in my writing." I returned to the first page, where I had drawn a honeycomb, lying on the ground where I found it—only there was no ground, no nearby tree in the drawing. Instead, the object floated on my page. "I'm realizing that I didn't show you much about my object," I said. "I didn't show where is it, what's around it. I'll do that now." I sketched the context in which I'd found the honeycomb.

"Writers, I hope you are realizing that when partners ask questions, like 'Where?' and 'How?' and 'Why?' then we can go back and think about how to put more information into our writing."

ACTIVE ENGAGEMENT

Guide partners in asking questions about each other's work.

"Partner 2, take out your writing first. Put it between you and Partner 1, and in a clear voice, read your first page to Partner 1. Listen *carefully*, Partner 1. Once Partner 2 is done reading, you are going to ask a question that will help Partner 2 say more about the information he or she is teaching. Go!"

As the children set to work, I called out little reminders.

"Think about what Partner 1 *didn't* tell you about this page. What information is missing?"

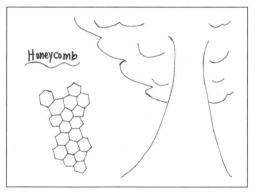

FIG. 9–1 Teachers drawing of the honeycomb with tree added for context.

"Ask a question that begins with 'where' or 'how' or 'why,' and don't forget to ask questions about the pictures and the words."

After a few minutes, I called out, "Stop, look, and listen."

Once I had the children's attention, I said, "I heard Liam ask his partner, 'Where do you ride your scooter?' That gave Mathew the idea that he could show the park in his writing! Now he's going to add trees and grass and the little fence that he scoots along. Tanisa asked her partner, 'Why is the dog on the leash?' and Emma said to keep her dog safe. And so Emma is going to write the word *safe*. Whoa! That's so important, because it means that Emma's book will teach people how to keep *their* dogs safe, too.

"Partner 1, your turn. Partner 2, sit on your writing and get ready to help Partner 1 think about more to add. What else are you dying to know that isn't yet on your partner's paper?"

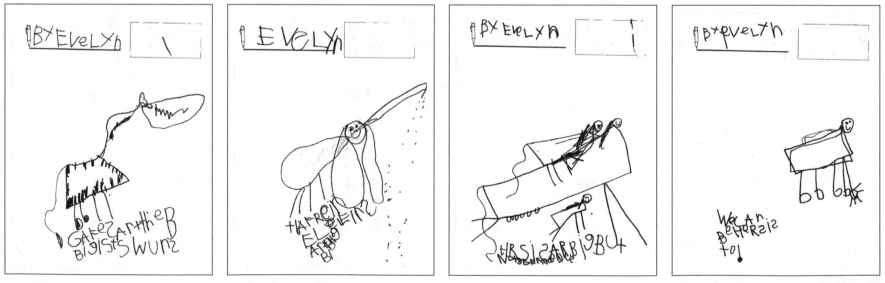

FIG. 9–2   Evelyn's writing: *Giraffes are the biggest ones.*
The friend elephants are big.
Horses are big but not bigger than us.
We can be horses, too!

LINK

Send the children off, reminding them that they have some choices about how to work on their books.

In a quiet and solemn voice, I asked the children to lean in close to me. "Writers, I want you to know how important this challenging work is—this work of asking and answering questions about a partner's writing. When we make teaching books, it is really important to include as much information as we need to help readers *learn* about our topics. But we might not always know if we included enough. Partners do an important job when they ask questions about what we have written. Then, when we answer them, it gives us ideas about what to add to our books! I am going to add that to our chart about revising. Right now, as you go off to your spot, think about how you might add on to your book. Think about the information that your partner asked questions about. If you need to hear the questions again before you go off to your writing spot, wait here on the rug with your partner to have a second try. And you might be ready to start a new piece, rather than adding on. You are the writier, so you'll have to decide and plan. If you are ready, show me by sitting up tall, folder in your lap, and eyes on me."

I sent off the children who felt ready to get to work and stayed on the rug a bit longer with the few partnerships who needed another chance to try asking and answering questions about each other's work.

Reflecting on Your Role in the Writing Conference

LUCILLE CLIFTON, one of this nation's greatest poets, once gave us advice that has changed everything we do. At a Teachers College Reading and Writing Project reunion, she said, "Nurture your imagination. You cannot create what you cannot imagine." That advice is as important for teachers as it for students, and it is important for your work with conferring and small groups (as well as for everything else). Teachers come into the profession with images of what it means to teach, images that have been formed through years—decades, even—of being students in classrooms. The writing workshop approach to conferring asks that teachers form new images of teaching, especially of what it means to provide feedback.

Today you might think about some of the assumptions that underlie your conferences and see if you can assess your own conferring, looking for ways your teaching is especially powerful and for ways it can get even stronger. You might start by watching yourself as you move among the students, giving them feedback. Especially when children are revising, it can be easy to fall into the trap of suggesting to the child exactly what ideas to add to make the book stronger. But Donald Murray, father of the writing process, suggests that it is best to talk to apprentice writers as if that person is a senior colleague. Because the writer is the author, he or she is the owner of the draft, the one with all the intentions and plans. As the teacher, you are the midwife, the coach, the assistant, but it is the writer—the child—who holds the reins. This is reflected in the fact that the author will ideally be the one to literally hold the paper and the pen. Then, too, it is the author who determines at least the starting topic of conversation. Although you will start things off by asking questions, the questions are broad enough that they essentially say to the writer, "Take us to your areas of concern." You ask, "What are you trying to do?" "How's it going?" "How can I help?" It is the writer's response to questions such as these that especially shapes the focus of the interaction.

This does *not* mean that you should refrain from teaching assertively and explicitly. What it means instead is that you should aim to teach the writer something she can do that will help her forever rather than aiming to fix up the piece of writing.

MID-WORKSHOP TEACHING
Being Our Own Writing Partner: Self-Assessing

"Hailey said something really interesting to her partner. She said, 'I am teaching you here about making a goal in soccer.' And then you know what she did? (Listen up because this is amazing.) She said something else *before* her partner even had a chance to ask her a question. She said, 'I am going to show you *where* to kick the ball. Right here in the corner is the best place.' Did you hear that, Super Writers? Hailey thought of her own question. And then she answered it all by herself! Writers, are you realizing that you can ask yourself the same questions you asked your partner? Are you thinking to yourselves as you write, '*How* does this work?' Or '*Where* does this happen?' Or '*What* more do I know that I could add?' Or 'Is this teaching what I want to teach?' See if you can ask yourself a question right now and try to answer it. Be your own writing partner, just like Hailey did."

As Students Continue Working . . .

"Writers, if you can't figure out what else to add to your books, be your own partner. Try asking yourself the same types of questions your partner asked you."

"If your page is getting filled up, you've probably got enough information. So go ahead and move on to your next page!"

"Are you using your words? Remember to be brave and use what you know to get a word down.

You'll be able to confer well if you consider your own experience with this sort of relationship. Your principal comes to observe your teaching and to give you feedback. She doesn't tell you, "Teach it this way." Rather, she asks, "What were you hoping to achieve?" and lets your answer guide the conversation. Your hairdresser observes your hair not to impose his vision, but to help you realize your own. Either way, the observer first needs to take lessons from you. "What have you been thinking?" they ask, "What should I watch for?"

As you watch yourself teaching, you might keep in mind a guideline that Donald Murray once gave to us. "Above all," he said, "In a good writing conference, a writer's energy for writing should go up, not down." Think of the times when someone has observed your teaching and given you feedback. What do you need from that interaction to increase your energy and motivation? You probably do not need or expect to be given a zillion compliments, but you hope that your observer believes in you—that you have the capacity to do great things, that you have promise as a teacher. When your observer sees and believes in what you can do, you believe in yourself. Sure, you have problems, challenges, and areas that merit more work. But your observer also sees your gifts and talks to you about them and sees, too, ways you can work to go from where you are to an exciting next level that is very much within your reach. You leave the interaction feeling like your efforts are paying off. If this is the sort of feedback you need, and if you keep this in mind when giving feedback to your students, your conferring will be incrementally better.

In this session you are helping students elaborate on their information and be able to say, explain, and ultimately teach more. Because it is your first unit of study, your students are learning what it means to write for other people—for an audience. You, the teacher, are usually the first to be able to respond to a piece of work. There will be conferences that help students clarify what they are saying in their writing. You will also want to coach youngsters and give them strategies that will help them say more, not just for now but so that they can transfer and apply it in other pieces of writing as well. Part of your work will be to support children in naming and reaching toward their intentions for their writing. To do any of this will require you to look closely at what your students are doing well so that your teaching builds form a place of strength.

So think about saying things like "I can see that you worked really hard on . . . " and "The way you . . . is so super. I have a feeling you are going to be famous for the way you do that!" Try to support a child's hard work, not her IQ or inborn talent. In other words, celebrate what children are able to decide to do (make an effort) rather than something they have no control over (being "smart"). You are going to want to praise children who don't give up, who use their strategies, and who are tenacious. Much research has shown that it is important for all of us to understand that our abilities reflect our effort, and we can work hard in ways that accelerate our abilities.

As this part of the unit begins to draw to an end, you might take time to reflect a bit on how *you* have changed, as well as how the kids have changed. This is a good time to set goals for yourself. In doing do, it can help to think a bit about what is especially essential in an effective conference.

Interviewing Writers about Their Process

Interview a child about his writing process. Then hand over the questioning to kids in the class for everyone to learn from.

"Writers, you'll notice that I have an extra chair next to me. That's my special writer's interview chair! Professional writers give interviews on the radio and on TV all the time. They answer questions about their writing process and about how they got their ideas. We can do that in our room, too. We can learn a lot from each other about not only *what* to write but also about *how* to write. Earlier, I asked Fabian if he'd be willing to be my guest today. Fabian, come on up and bring your book with you." Fabian made his way to the front of the room and sat in the chair facing mine, writing in hand (see Figure 9–3). "I'm going to start off our questions, and then I'll turn the mike over to the audience." I held up a pencil, microphone-style, to my mouth and said, "Tell us, Fabian, what drew you to writing about boats?" Then I handed him the pencil.

"Well, I uh . . . I wrote about boats because I go on the ferry boat all the time to go see my grandpa."

"Aha! So you wrote about this topic because you actually ride on boats like ferries. Thinking about things that you do is a great way to find topics. I see the boat here and the windows, and this is a passenger, right? How do you make your pictures so clear?"

"I close my eyes like this. And I concentrate really hard on what it looks like, and then I just draw it."

"Let me see if I'm understanding what you're saying. You close your eyes and concentrate on what you see, like the shapes and colors. You get a really clear picture in your head, and then you draw that."

"Yep. See here are the life jackets. I saw those when I closed my eyes."

"What an important detail to add. Writers, we are learning a lot from today's guest writer Fabian, about things we too can try. I'm turning the mike over to you now. Give me a thumbs up if you have a question for Fabian."

After a few questions from the class, I said, "Writers, you can interview each other whenever you want to learn about another writer's process—and then you can try out the things you hear that spark ideas for your own writing."

FIG. 9–3   This is Fabian's first page of his book about boats. Fabian has added details such as the wind, water, and life jackets to this page. (Labels: *Ferry boat. Life jacket. Windy day.*)

Stretching Out Words to Write Even More Sounds

I N AN EARLIER SESSION, you encouraged children to listen to the first sound they heard in a word and to record that sound. Now you'll give them strategies to hear *past* the first sound. In this minilesson, you will demonstrate how writers decide what they'll write, isolate the first word, say it and stretch it out, write the first sound, reread it, and listen for more sounds until the word is satisfactorily represented on the page. You'll also teach children how an alphabet chart can help them locate letters for sounds they have not yet internalized.

Regardless of whether children are writing sentences or labels, in this minilesson, you'll need to demonstrate saying each word slowly *within a sentence* and rereading the sentence as it grows on the page, the same way you reread a word as you add more sounds. In making this process explicit for children, you're increasing their phonemic awareness and solidifying their understanding of the difference between words and letters.

This lesson assumes most children are representing words with a combination of initial consonants and some random letter strings. For more experienced writers, you might modify this so that you demonstrate how different strategies are used with different words.

Children need frequent and varied instruction in sound-letter correspondence to write the letters they need. During other times of the day you'll teach children to study, admire, and talk about the letters in their names; you'll sing the alphabet song, notice environmental print, and collect items that begin with certain sounds; you'll teach children a few precious sight words such as *me* and *mom*. Meanwhile, in the writing workshop, you'll teach children that letters can spell the messages they're dying to get across. In other words, writing workshop is where children will purposefully and meaningfully apply the letter and sound knowledge that you teach them explicitly in other parts of your day.

In this session, you'll teach children that to record more sounds in words, they must say each word slowly, listening to each part of the word, and reread often.

IN THIS SESSION, you'll teach students that young writers say words slowly, over and over again, to write all of the sounds that they hear.

GETTING READY

- ✔ Physical items in the classroom to incorporate into a song about letter sounds (see Teaching and Active Engagement)

- ✔ Enlarged alphabet chart with each child's name printed next to the letter with which it begins. Children should already be familiar with this chart (see Teaching).

- ✔ Copy of alphabet chart for each child to have on hand while writing (see Teaching and Active Engagement)

- ✔ Your teaching book on honeycombs that you introduced the day before (see Teaching and Active Engagement)

- ✔ Materials for children to use during the share—white boards or individual paper, Post-its, and writing utensils

Stretching Out Words to Write Even More Sounds

CONNECTION

Start the meeting with a phonemic awareness warm-up song.

"Stop, look, and listen," I sang, and the children joined me in the response: "Oh yeah!" Now that I had their full attention, I leaned forward as if to tell them something, and instead sang, to the tune of "Twinkle Twinkle Little Star," "I see something in the room/That begins with the sound /r/," and I gestured just a bit toward the rabbit. Now, bringing that into the song and gesturing for children to sing with me, I sang, "I see something in the room/ That begins with the sound /r/ rabbit, /p/ . . . ?"

The children called out "Plant" and "Pen," and I scooped one of those up and returned to the song. "I see something in the room/That begins with the sound /r/ rabbit, /p/ plant." We continued in this way for a few more rounds of the song, incorporating a few more sounds.

❖ **Name the teaching point.**

"Today I want to teach you that brave writers need lots of practice in hearing sounds and matching them to letters. To get the letters down, writers say the word they want to write, stretching it like a rubber band. Then they record the first sound they hear and reread. Then they stretch the word out again to hear the next sound. And so on and so on."

TEACHING

Tell children that there is a new tool—a mini alphabet chart—waiting at their writing spots.

I held up a small version of the class alphabet chart, handling it as if it were precious. "Writers, I've put little alphabet charts like this one next to each of your writing spots. You've seen the big one hanging on our wall, and some of you have even used it to help you write words in your books. It seems to me that you are ready to have your very own! Watch now while I show you how I use this very helpful tool."

When you teach young children something technical—like matching letters and sounds—it can help to introduce an attention-grabbing device, like a singing game.

Write publicly, demonstrating what you want children to try.

"I am going to add to my book about the honeycomb. This page shows the honeycomb lying on the ground, where I found it. The next page shows a swarm of bees around the honeycomb. Bees make honeycombs. And the last page shows a person licking honey off a spoon. People eat the honey bees make. Yum! My book so far goes like this."

> Today on the way to school I found a honeycomb.
> It looks really weird.
> It is a bee's house.

"I need to add words to some of these pages. Let's see. I'll add some words to my new page that shows all the honeybees making the honeycomb. Watch how I stretch out some words."

Shifting into the role of a child, I said, "Umm . . . I think I'll start with the words *honey bees*. That's the whole idea, but first I have to hear the sounds in just the first word—*honey*: honey. /h/." I muttered. "Hhhhh like *hat*. Let me look for the hat on my alphabet chart. Ooh! Here it is! The hat has an *H*! Hhhhoney starts like hhhhat. *H*. Let me reread," which I did, with my finger under my print. I then articulated the still-unwritten sounds "'onnnnn' /n/ like *nest*! Let me find it! *N!*" I wrote it and reread, "honnneeeeee *E* like *eagle*! Did you see what I did? Now I'm going to reread *again*. 'Honey.' See how I keep rereading after I add each sound that I hear? Now what comes next? Bees. I'm going to stretch it out the same way. Watch how I use the alphabet chart." Breaking it down, I said, "/b/" and wrote *b*. I again reread with my finger under the letter *e*, and soon I'd progressed to saying /b, /e/." I wrote *be* and again reread.

"Did you notice how first I said all of what I wanted to write—*honey bees?* Then I broke it down to just the first word—*honey*. Then I wrote and reread that. Then I said the next word—*bees*. I stretched out the sounds, wrote the letters, and again I reread. I reread after each letter I wrote, but I also reread all the words when I was done with the whole idea. Writers reread a *lot*. We reread as we stretch the sounds in a word, and we reread each word in a whole idea."

ACTIVE ENGAGEMENT

Ask children to join you in writing the sounds you hear in the words you write.

"Will you help me keep going? First I'll reread what I wrote. Let's do that together." I waited for the class to be with me, and together, with my finger under the print, we read, "'Honey bees.' Now can you help me write 'big buzz,' 'cause boy, do bees get noisy when they make honeycomb. What's first? *Big*. Let's say it and then find the first letter you hear on your alphabet chart! /b/. That's an easy one! *B!* Like *bee!* On your hands," I pointed to the palm of my hand, "pretend to write that word and I'll do it up here." I wrote *b*. "Now what do we do? We reread, don't we? Let's do it together. 'b/i/g ' /iii/ like *igloo*! Look for it on your chart and hold it up! Let's reread. 'Bi/g/.' /g/ like . . ." I let my voice trail off and waited until children called out, "Goat!" "Yes! the *G!*" I cheered them on, "Find it! Point to it! Now draw it on your hand.

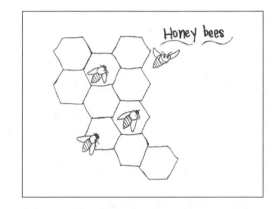

FIG. 10–1 Teacher's drawing of a swarm of bees around the honeycomb with the words "honey bees" added.

"Let's reread: 'Big.' What comes next? Buzz. Stretch out the first sound. Find the letter that you hear. It's like typing! Find and point to the first sound /bbbb/. Hold up your charts! Bbbbbuzz like *bee* again!

"Say it with me," I said. "We are stretching the word like a rubber band." After saying buuuuuuuzz together a few times, I said, "What sound do you hear next? /u/? Okay. We hear an /u/ sound. Point to it on your chart, write it on your hand, and I'll write it." Soon we had added *buz* to the other words on the page. "What should we do next?" I asked. "Read the whole idea!" a few children replied. "Yes, you remembered! Let's reread what we just wrote together. 'Big buzz.' Yes!

"We got lucky with that last word. You all are letter *b* experts by now! Let's try a few more words of my book before you go off to work on your own. 'Swarm.' A swarm is a group of bees." I helped children stretch and hear the sounds in *swarm* and then gave them the word *spoon* to try on their own.

LINK

Tell children to try on their own what you have done together, reminding them of the many available tools for matching letters to sounds.

"Today you are going to have some more writing time, and I want to suggest that instead of working on whatever is your most recent book, you look through all of your books and choose your favorite because in our next writing workshop, we are going to have a publishing celebration. We're going to display our books like art in a museum. And guess who's going to visit our museum? The fifth-graders!"

The kids' mouths opened wide.

"We want to be sure the big kids know what information you're teaching in your pictures, be sure to get down as many words as we can in your favorite book. Think you're up for that? I do.

"Today, as you go off to write, remember that writers not only fill their pages up with pictures, they *also* fill their pages up with words. Getting more sounds onto the page (more letters in your words) will help you remember what it is that you wrote and will help readers understand you. And remember, you have several tools to help you write words. You can look at the alphabet chart I just gave you, but also at the name chart and at all the words around our room."

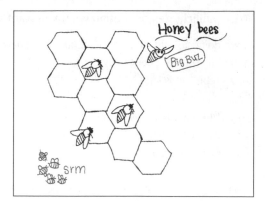

FIG. 10–2 Teacher's drawing of a swarm of bees around the honeycomb with the words "swarm" and "big buzz" added.

Students whose labels contain enough letters that both you and they can somewhat decipher them are more than ready to start writing sentences on each page. You could keep the small group of them with you on the carpet and say, "I've noticed that all of you have been working hard to add words to your pictures and that many of you have tried to label, like in Freight Train. *That is wonderful. I did some labeling, just like Donald Crews did in* Freight Train, *also. In this piece I am teaching people about things they need before they go to bed. I have labels, but now I want to stretch myself as a writer and add a whole idea—a sentence. I think I'll write, "'You need a toothbrush.' That is something you need before you go to bed! You need to brush your teeth, right?" After you model this in your own writing, you could say, "I'm wondering how many of you feel that you could stretch yourselves as writers today and try adding some sentences under the pictures. Raise your hands if you think you can. Terrific! I can't wait to see your work!"*

Helping Writers of Varying Abilities to Put Words on Their Paper

IT IS IMPORTANT TO CONTINUE to help children identify what they want to say, isolate their first word, say that word slowly, and record the sounds they hear. Most children will need individual help with this. Don't feel that your teaching has fallen on deaf ears when children continue to need support. Do try to release your support by encouraging children to be the word stretchers in a conference, rather than having them listen to you stretching the words as they record the sounds. Take a little step back and notice the flow of your room now. You've raised the stakes and probably made some writers feel needy. Don't push your writers so hard that they can no longer carry on with independence and engagement. If your children start to become dependent, you won't be free to do the teaching you need to do. Remind them to stretch their words, write what they hear, and be brave!

One way children will cope with the challenge of adding more words to their writing is to copy print from the classroom, write only what they know they can spell, or use similar strategies that feel safe. Continue to focus on choosing a topic that writers know and care about, drawing the content first, talking about the idea aloud, and only then writing. This will help them remember that their message—the meaning they want to communicate—is still central to the act of writing.

(continues)

MID-WORKSHOP TEACHING **Stretching Out Words to Hear Beginning and Ending Sounds**

"I was watching Draco write about his parrot, and he was trying to write *parrot*. He forgot how to write the /t/ sound, so guess what he did? He looked on the name chart and thought, 'Is there a name that starts like the /t/ sound? Oh! *Tom* starts like the /t/ sound.' Then Draco wrote the letter *t* at the end of the word *parrot*. So writers, you can find sounds for letters on the chart just like Draco did.

"Draco didn't just stop at parrot, though. He remembered that to teach things well means using lots of words, so he looked at his picture and realized he'd drawn a cage that needed a label, and also the pellets that he feeds his parrot. *And* he wanted to write that his parrot talks—that it repeats certain things he says. I bet you know what he did next, right? You got it! Draco pulled out his name chart again and found names that begin with the same sounds as the words he wanted to write. And now look!" I held up Draco's piece for all the kids to see. "Draco's managed to teach us all about his parrot because he's added all these words to his pictures."

As Students Continue Working . . .

"Put your alphabet charts right next to you as you write, so when you say the words and are thinking about the letters, you have them right there next to you!"

"Point to something new and stretch out all the sounds. Don't just write down one! Write down a bunch!"

"Count the labels that you made on one page! Who has five or more? Who has three? Try to get one or two more and then turn the page! Keep going!"

This is a good time to collect writing folders and look them over, sorting children into groups based on their approach to print. Some, like Deleana, will write with random strings of letters (see Figure 10–3). Though it can be hard to determine much from the piece of writing itself, you can gather a lot of useful information by sitting with the writer as she writes or by talking to her about what she has done. You will need to observe how a writer reads the random strings of letters. Does she have a sense that texts are read left to right, top to bottom? Does she seem to think that more marks on the page means a longer utterance? When she "reads" a message, does it sound like a written text, or does it sound conversational? Is the text stable, so that each time she "rereads" it, the text says roughly the same things? Do you see sight words or nonrandom spellings hidden within the strings? Is the text, in fact, not random at all, but just squeezed together into a big line that appears random? Only in the presence of the writer can these questions be answered.

To learn more, I'd want to ask her if the big figure in the picture is her mom and get her to say "mom" slowly and record the first sound—because I have a hunch she could do so just fine! I would also want to coach Deleana to teach us about her mom or about moms in general. This way she can also work on the language of explanatory texts.

Jordan (see Figure 10–4) is clearly in a different place than Deleana when it comes to print. His approximations are quite conventional. It's intriguing that he spells concrete concepts (*apple*, *lunch*, and *outside*) correctly, whereas abstract words (*then* and *had*) are more of a stretch. Because Jordan's spelling is this well developed, he may be ready to concentrate on using mostly lowercase letters. More significantly, he seems to think that writing involves captioning pictures. ("This is the lunch. I am having bread."). In this part of the unit, I want to encourage Jordan to teach more about the food and lunch time and less about the story. I will want to keep my eye on this to see if he starts to use a different kind of writing voice in the second part of this unit, when we shift to narrative writing.

FIG. 10–3   Deleana's writing: *My mom said, "Cut it out." My mom said, "Cut it out." My mom said, "Cut it out." I love my mom. I love my mom.*

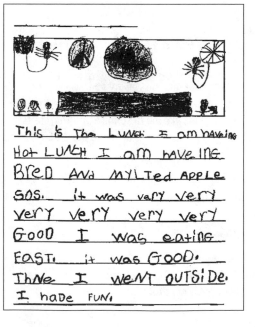

FIG. 10–4   Jordan's writing: *This is the lunch. I am having hot lunch. I am having bread and my little applesauce. It was very very very very very good. I was eating fast. It was good. Then I went outside. I had fun.*

Using High-Frequency Words When Writing

Recruit children's help adding high-frequency words to labels around the room.

I gathered white boards, markers, and blank Post-its and convened the class.

"Writers, do you know that not one of you has tugged on my sleeve to ask for help writing words today? You've been too busy figuring it out on your own! Some of you used your name charts to write words, and others of you used your alphabet charts, and lots of you used both.

"But do you know what? Even though those tools are super helpful, you don't always need them. That's because there are some words that all of you know even *without* looking at your word tools. They are stuck like glue to your memories! Words like *a*, *the*, *me*, and *my*. I see those words dancing across your pages.

"I'm thinking that our classroom could use your help. Look around the room. We have so many things labeled—the door, the library, our pet rabbit, our science center, even our chairs! But most of those things have one-word labels like 'door' or 'chair.'

"Everyone, let's read the words that I have here on our easel. They are the same words that are on our word wall." I held up a little pile of note cards on which I'd written the high-frequency words students had been practicing and learning.

I pointed and they read, "The." "Let's shout out the letters we see in 'the.' Give me a *T!*"

"*T!*"
"Give me an *H!*"
"*H!*"
"Give me an *E!*"
"*E!*"

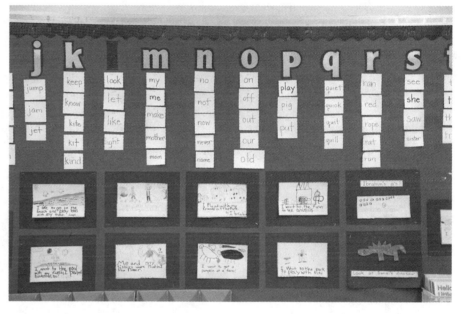

FIG. 10–5   Part of a high-frequency word chart

"What does that spell?"

"The!" we all shouted together.

"Matthew, quickly find something in the room that you can add 'the' to and write it in nice neat letters with this marker on this Post-it note. Everyone else, write it on your white board. Caps off. Go! When you're done, check the letters up here on the easel and then hold up your boards!"

Matthew scrambled to the door.

"The door!" I called out. "Nice choice. Read it back, Mathew. Put your fingers under the words."

I called a few kids more kids up and soon the room had some longer labels that read: "the door," "a rug," "the library," "a rabbit," and "a cage."

"Wow! All these words everywhere. Our room is getting written, just like our books!"

Ask children to add a word they know by heart to their writing. Call on them to share what they've added.

"Right now, take out your writing and see if you can find a place to add one of the little words we know by heart. When you've found a place, show the person sitting next to you.

"Writers, when I point to you, hold up your book and read us your new label."

As I called on them, children sang out, "The sun!" "My mom." "A ball." "My cat and dog."

"Before we end our meeting, grab a marker off your table and add the word *my* to the label 'chair' on your seat." Soon the chairs all read "my chair."

"Wow, you brave, brave writers! Let me just point this out in case you are not aware of how amazing this is. You have written so many words using so many tools. You have gotten a bunch of words stuck in your memory like glue, and you have stretched out sounds to write words you *don't* have stuck in your memory like glue. When you are five, you don't know every single word yet. You're not supposed to. But you *are* supposed to be brave and use tools. And that's what you all are doing!"

Making Writing the Best It Can Be

Dear Teachers,

As you opened to today's session, you might have expected to find a specific minilesson. Our decades of work with millions of children have taught us what to include in a curriculum like this one, and each session reflects our collective experience. One important thing we have learned along the way is that classes can differ quite a bit and that teachers have a lot of wisdom about what their students need. Today, rather than including a minilesson, we write you a letter of suggestions and ideas describing how we might proceed at this point in the unit. We will be doing this throughout these units of study, with the hope that this will give you a welcome opportunity to begin writing your own curriculum, tailoring it to the particular students you teach. Here, we will offer up our best suggestions to help you imagine possibilities.

At this point in the unit, the children have spent two or three weeks working on their information books. It is time to celebrate all they've learned, bringing their writing to an audience outside of you and their classmates before they move forward to the next bend in the unit (where they will turn to writing narratives). By now, they have picked the piece they'd like to publish. Today you might teach that writers pause before they finish a piece, deciding if they are truly finished, perhaps by using a checklist. Then, you can explain, writers add some final touches, and finally, they fancy up the writing for publication. The checklist that follows reinforces all of the behaviors you have been teaching. You will want to guide your students in reflecting on these pieces of writing, naming what they are doing well as writers of informational texts.

After the writing time in workshop today, an extended share can allow for youngsters to present their work to other children in the school. Your children can have their first "formal" writing audience of the year! At the end of this first unit, as you may know, you will prepare a more elaborate publication celebration. This one is simply to mark the end of the time writing information books and to help children know that writers write to share their work with readers. Here is one way all this can happen in workshop today.

MINILESSON

Generally, the connection in a minilesson is meant to remind children of what they have recently learned and to help them propel this learning forward into subsequent days. Today you might ask them to turn to a partner and try to remember one thing they have learned to do as writers for each finger on a hand. Then you can share what you overheard them saying, to help solidify some of the writing strategies they've learned in the unit so far. It might be things like the following:

- Think of something you know and can teach others about.

- Picture it in your head to remember the details.

- Add details to your pictures and your words.

- Use the alphabet cards and environmental print.

- Stretch out your words and write letters for the sounds you hear.

Tell them that they will each be selecting a piece of writing to share with visitors who will come at the end of the hour. Say that these visitors will need as many words—as much help—as possible to be able to understand and appreciate these wonderful information books. As writers, they'll need to use all that they know.

Then you can add a new strategy to figure out what to do when you feel done. "Today I want to teach you something about publishing your writing. Before authors finish, they do everything they know to make their writing the best that it can be! You have been checking your teaching books to make sure you've added words and pictures. You all have done a great job of checking for those things—But guess what! Authors check for *more* things; they use a checklist to help them, just like the one I have right here! Today I'm going to give each of you your own copy of this checklist to use before you publish, just the way other authors use them. Little by little, you can add to this checklist, so it can always help you as you are finishing a piece of writing, even as you grow as a writer!"

You will need to create some icons to help children be able to decode—or, more likely, remember— each item on the checklist. (See the online resources for a full-size, reproducible version of the checklist shown on page 83.)

For the teaching portion of the minilesson, you can demonstrate using this checklist with a piece of your own writing, being sure the writing will reveal things from the checklist you have done, things you have done a little, and things you can try to do next. After you offer up this very short demonstration, as always, you can debrief, pointing out what you did that you hope the children will learn to do. Remember, you don't need to take the time to do the work that the checklist indicates needs doing right there in front of the students. That would make the demonstration far too long! Instead, you only need to demonstrate *using* the checklist to help plan the writing work each child will do during writing time today to get ready to publish and celebrate with the fifth-grade audience. It might be wise to have a piece of writing that calls for several revisions, based on the checklist, yet demonstrate choosing only one to name as your plan for the day. That way, children are less likely to feel overwhelmed if their piece has several kinds of revision called for by the checklist.

After you have demonstrated using the checklist with one piece of writing, ask the children to try it, using their own writing. Have them look over the writing they've selected for publication and use the checklist to make a plan for the writing work that needs doing before the celebration. They may run through the list and say that they have done everything. Remind them that they are *looking* for something to work on. Everyone will find at least one thing! You might read the checklist or just the first few things on it out loud to remind kids to look for those things with their partner. Ask partnerships to try this together with one person's writing. This should only take a moment or so, and they needn't finish, as long as they have the opportunity to work through more than one item on the checklist. As they talk, listen in and help some of the partnerships understand how to do this work. If any children have an interesting idea about using this checklist that would be helpful to the whole class, you might want to share that work with everyone, after you have called for their attention again.

When you send children off to work, remind them of the choices they have as they prepare their books for today's mini-celebration. Some of them may decide to add more labels or sentences. Others may decide to add pages. Some may decide to do some of the work that their checklist helped them remember to do—and they may need to spend some time finishing using the checklist! Yet others may decide they need to remove pages that don't belong, perhaps replacing these with pages that add to their topic. You may want to send them off to work in stages, based on what it is they plan to do today. This will encourage children to be intentional and purposeful with their writing. Send them off to work by saying, "Those of you who will be doing . . . , get started." Then, as that group goes off, "Those of you who will be doing . . . , go ahead and get started." As the final send off, you may want to say, "Those of you who are not sure of your plan

Information Writing Checklist

	Kindergarten	NOT YET	STARTING TO	YES!	Grade 1	NOT YET	STARTING TO	YES!
	Structure				**Structure**			
Overall	I told, drew, and wrote about a topic.	☐	☐	☐	I taught my readers about a topic.	☐	☐	☐
Lead	I told what my topic was.	☐	☐	☐	I named my topic in the beginning and got my readers' attention.	☐	☐	☐
Transitions	I put different things I knew about the topic on my pages.	☐	☐	☐	I told different parts about my topic on different pages.	☐	☐	☐
Ending	I had a last part or page.	☐	☐	☐	I wrote an ending.	☐	☐	☐
Organization	I told, drew, and wrote information across pages.	☐	☐	☐	I told about my topic part by part.	☐	☐	☐
	Development				**Development**			
Elaboration	I drew and wrote important things about the topic.	☐	☐	☐	I put facts in my writing to teach about my topic.	☐	☐	☐
Craft	I told, drew, and wrote some details about the topic.	☐	☐	☐	I used labels and words to give facts.	☐	☐	☐
	Language Conventions				**Language Conventions**			
Spelling	I could read my writing.	☐	☐	☐	I used all I knew about words and chunks (*at, op, it,* etc.) to help me spell.	☐	☐	☐
	I wrote a letter for the sounds I heard.	☐	☐	☐	I spelled the word wall words right and used the word wall to help me spell other words.	☐	☐	☐
	I used the word wall to help me spell.	☐	☐	☐				

yet, please stay here and I can help you make a plan." This, then, collects all the children who need a little more time and allows you to give them the support they need.

CONFERRING AND SMALL-GROUP WORK

Conferring today may be a bit more clear-cut since many of your children named a specific goal for today's work to prepare for the mini-celebration. As you crouch down near them, ask children, "So, how are you getting your writing ready for the celebration today? What last minute changes and touch-ups did you decide it needs?" Let their answers guide your teaching.

Another goal of today's conferring is to bring some excitement and energy into the celebration. This is the reason that writers write—to bring their work into the world. Let children revel in their plans to showcase their work. Let yourself "ooh" and "ah" and marvel at the risks they've taken and the growth they've shown. Find ways to name the hard work children have done, and point out to them the changes you are seeing in their writing. For example, I might highlight how Draco has made such a long book and has remembered to draw and write words on all his pages (see Figure 11–1) or how Clarissa has given the

FIG. 11–1   Draco's writing: *Reading workshop. We read books. These are people. These are the books. (Labels: People. Books.)*

Writing workshop time. (Label: Reading.)

We use the computers. (Label: Computers.)

We go to recess. The slide. (Label: Slide.)

reader detailed information about cats in the sentences that she wrote (see Figure 11–2). To help them honor and value their work, you might suggest ways to fancy up the finished work: adding covers, bylines, title pages, borders, or dedications. Encourage children who are done with one book to look back at others in their folder. Maybe they can present two of their books to the fifth-graders!

MID-WORKSHOP TEACHING

In your mid-workshop teaching, near the end of the work time, you might suggest that kids take a few moments to practice reading their books aloud to their partner, making sure to read in a clear voice and to point to any important pictures as they read. The listening partner can make suggestions and offer a compliment. In this way, students will be preparing for their fifth-grade visitors, getting themselves ready to present their work while simultaneously hearing any final tips of things to add to their books that they may have not noticed themselves.

SHARE

The mini-celebration will be an extended share session that might last ten or fifteen minutes. We suggest you invite an older grade—we asked fifth-graders for this particular class—to come view your class's collection of books. Although this won't be an extended event, you will want it to feel momentous to your kids. Position each of your writers/teachers around the room so that the visiting students can easily pair themselves with a kindergartner. The kindergartners can read aloud their books to each of their visitors, and then the fifth-graders can give a compliment before moving on to hear and admire another book. That is, each student will read his or her piece several times to different fifth-grade visitors. You may want to group the kids around the room according to topic. Maybe one area is for books about family, another for books about pets, another for books about activities, and so on. Invite your students to help make big, colorful signs that direct their visitors to the different kinds of books in the room. Whatever you decide, make sure the event feels celebratory.

After the celebration, display the work for all to see. You will then need to do a bit of housekeeping in children's writing folders. One option is to clip together, or just remove, the pieces that they have done so far. They will be turning from teaching books to stories in the next part of the unit and may need an empty folder to keep the distinction clear. Do not send these pieces of writing home yet, though. You will want to use them at the end of the unit to help kids reflect on how they have grown, and you will be returning to them in the next unit, *Writing for Readers*.

Good luck!

Lucy and Amanda

FIG. 11–2 Clarissa's writing: *I love my cat. I love my cat when he runs in the house. Then he snarls.*

I pet my cat on his back. He purrs. He and me.

My cat sits on my lap. My cat runs away.

Getting Ideas for Stories and Practicing Storytelling

IN THIS SESSION, you'll teach students that writers get ready to write by telling their stories first.

GETTING READY

✔ Trays full of rolls of tape and ready-made booklets made of three or four sheets of paper stapled together. (You'll want to make several booklets, each using whatever kinds of paper your children have been using.)

✔ Ready-made large booklet and marker for your demonstration

✔ A picture book with a simple, lively storyline and with speech bubbles or short bits of dialogue that you will use during this bend as a mentor story. (Here we refer to *Creak! Said the Bed*, but many other beloved stories will work just as well.) Read the whole book aloud to the class ahead of time.

✔ A story about something that happened to the whole class that you will write and reference throughout this bend

✔ "When We Are Done, We Have Just Begun" chart (see Mid-Workshop Teaching)

✔ Writing folders (see Share)

✔ Student writing samples for modeling (see Share)

SOME CHILDREN will come to school with a strong background in storytelling, while others will not have had that experience. Literary scholar Shirley Brice Heath says the most important thing an adult can do to support a child's literacy is to immerse the child in a culture of storytelling. Parents are naturals at scaffolding children to re-create events. For instance, a child and her dad return from the park, and the mother says, "What did you do at the park?" The child says, "I swinged," and the mother replies, "Did you?! Did Daddy push you on the swings?" The child nods and says, "Daddy pushed me and I go high. I touched the tree." The mother nods and retells the story. "Wow. Daddy pushed you on the swing! You went so high that you touched the leaves of the tree." This re-creation of the story is essential to learning how a sentence in standard English should sound and supports a child's ability to write stories in a clear and cohesive way.

In this part of the unit you will now be teaching your students to write stories instead of writing teaching books. Most state standards expect young children to recognize and create both informational texts and narratives, so now is a perfect time to draw your young writers' attention to the differences in structure and purpose of these two text types as they begin to explore storytelling. The standards emphasize the importance of narrating a sequence of events and describing a reaction or feeling in response to the events of that story. The language of the standards may feel too elevated or abstract for youngsters, but in this unit you are guiding them through the curriculum in a way that suits young writers perfectly. Just as you did with teaching books, you will emphasize features of the genre of story. This will help students tell stories from their lives in increasingly powerful ways. The foundation you create in this unit will support their growth through the units that follow.

Oral rehearsal (storytelling) will do wonders to help your young writers develop a sense of storybook language. Then too, you'll want to help children recognize the ways that this new form of writing parallels what they've already learned to do. Storytellers, like the authors of teaching books, plan for what they'll write and then use pictures and words to put that story on the page. Storytellers have the same kinds of strategies for adding more, stretching out words, and working with partners. Most importantly, all kinds of writers are independent and resourceful.

"The most important thing an adult can do to support a child's literacy is to immerse the child in a culture of storytelling."

Today you'll help children recall events the class has experienced together and spin those events into oral stories. You will show your students that writers take the events of their lives and shape those events into stories. Even the smallest, seemingly insignificant events can become powerful stories. We need only the tools to make them so.

Getting Ideas for Stories and Practicing Storytelling

CONNECTION

Tell children that now they will learn to write a different kind of book—stories—and ask them to notice what a story does as you read aloud the beginning of *Creak! Said the Bed*.

"Writers, long, long ago when we started our writing workshop, I showed you two different kinds of books by two very special authors. We have written teaching books like one of them." I held up *Freight Train*. "And today, we are going to start to learn how to write like the other." I held up *Creak! Said the Bed*. "We are going to write not teaching books, but stories—*true* stories from our lives.

"We just read this story together yesterday, but listen carefully now as I read just the beginning of *Creak! Said the Bed*. See if you can hear how a book that tells a story sounds different from a teaching book."

I read in my best storyteller's voice:

> *One dark night in the middle of the night, Momma and Papa were snoozing in bed.*
>
> *SQUEAK, went the door.*
>
> *And Evie said, "I'm scared in my room. Can I come in with you?"*
>
> *Poppa said, Snore,*
>
> *and Momma said, "Sure! There's plenty of room for Evie in the bed."*
>
> *So Evie bounced in.*

Invite children to help you describe what the author of this story does on the first page to pull readers in.

"What do you see the author doing on this page? I hear characters talking. We didn't hear characters talking in our teaching books! This is one way stories are different from teaching books. Let's think about *other* ways stories sound different.

"I see them doing things like . . ." I jumped up and down in my chair.

Teachers, you need not use this particular book if you don't have it. What is important is that you use a book that is (or could be) a true story that is ordinary enough that children feel they could have written it. It also needs to have an opening that feels like a story and sets the mood, rather than one that feels like an explanation or a list. Make sure the author has done things the children can try, too—like incuding speaking or noises or descriptions of the weather.

"Bounce!" the kids called out.

"And . . ." I closed my eyes, put my head in my hands, and snored.

"Snore!" the kids called out, giggling.

"And . . ." I made a squeaky door sound and a door opening gesture with my hand.

"Squeak!" the kids shouted out, delighted.

"You heard the same things I heard! So in stories, characters *talk* and they *do* things. Put your thumb on your knee if you felt like you were in that room, tucked into that big ol' bed." Lots of thumbs went on knees.

"Stories have the power to pull readers in like that. Good stories make readers feel like they are right there in the story, living it. When we get to hear the characters talk or see them do stuff, it helps us feel like we are right there. I bet we could learn to write like that!"

❖ **Name the teaching point.**

"Today I want to teach you that one way writers get ready to write true stories is to first practice telling the stories. They tell all the little things that happened, including what people said and did."

TEACHING

Tell a story of something that happened to the class to model how a story sounds.

"So what story could I tell? I need an idea. Hmm, . . . What is something that happened that I want to tell about? Oh, I know! The fire drill! That happened to *all* of us just the other day, remember?

"Listen as I tell the story. As I do, notice the way I tell this. It won't sound like a teaching book. It will sound like a story—like 'One time when . . .'"

Switching out of the role of teacher and into the role of storyteller, I said,

> One sunny day, all the kindergartners were reading in reading workshop. The room was quiet when all of a sudden—"Dong Dong Dong" went the bell!
>
> I called out, "Kindergartners, push in your chairs and line up at the door!"
>
> Everyone stood up, pushed in their chairs, and lined up at the door. I opened the door and out into the hall we went. Lots of other classes were heading down the hall toward the stairs. Our feet went clickity clack, clickity clack on the stairs, until we reached the lobby. We went outside and waited for the "all

As often as possible, we add a little drama to our minilessons and elicit children's participation. We do this not just for fun, but with the knowledge that active involvement promotes learning.

clear." We waited and waited and waited. Finally, the principal blew her whistle and said, "All clear!"
We walked back inside and walked upstairs to our classroom.

"Did you hear how I told our story from beginning to end? And how I said so many of the little things that happened? I didn't just say, 'We had a fire drill.' No way! That wouldn't be a story! Something I did to make it a story was tell what people did, like when I told how you all pushed in your chairs, and what people said, like when the principal said 'All clear!' I bet you could do those things, too."

ACTIVE ENGAGEMENT

Set partners up to tell the same class story from their perspective, remembering to tell every little thing that happened and to use their best storyteller's voices.

"Let's try something new. Turn to face your partner. Good. Now, using your best storyteller voices, tell the story of the fire drill together with your partner. Here's how you'll do it. Partner 1 will say one line, then Partner 2 will say the second line, then Partner 1 will say the next line, then it will be Partner 2's turn, and you'll keep telling each other the story like that until our class is out on that curb. Tell it the way you remember it. Where were you when the bell rang? What did you do or say? What happened next? Remember to tell all the little things that happened and to use your best storyteller's voices. Go!"

I listened in as the kids talked, and after a few minutes, I sang, "Stop, look, and listen!"

Recruit one partnership to tell their version of the story and point out all the things they did to tell this story well.

Then I called one partnership to the front of the room and asked them to tell their version of the fire drill.

As they took turns telling line after line, I prompted them as needed.

I was reading about turtles when the bell went Dong Dong Dong!

It was loud and scary.

You *told us to line up.*

We held hands.

We went into the hall.

Then we went outside.

We waited and waited. Then the principal blew the whistle.

Then it was over.

"Writers, did you notice what *they* just did? Casey and Joseline's story didn't just go, 'The bell rang and we went outside, the end,' did it? No way! Casey and Joseline told us about all the little things that happened between the moment the bell rang and when our class was standing on the curb. They even included how they felt. That's what writers do to tell a good story."

LINK

Ask children to come up with an idea for their story before you send them off to write.

"In our writing center are little booklets that you can take to write your stories, and there are rolls of tape, too. Just like when you wrote teaching books, you can make a story book or a story scroll. Before you get your supplies, close your eyes and get an idea for writing. You might think about something that happened to you today. Or you might think about something that happened to you over the weekend. Or something that happened with your really good friend. Or some other event you remember very well. Pick one idea, think about one time you did something, and get started. When you have it, put your thumb on your knee.

"Everyone who is going to write about something that happened last weekend, off you go.

"Everyone who is going to write about something you did at home, off you go!

"Everyone who is going to write about one time you did something with a friend, off you go!

"Everyone who is going to write about something that happened here, at school, off you go!"

FIG. 12-1 Yatri's writing: *One day I was at school with my friend.* (Labels: *Teacher. Table. Chair. Door. PS 199. Hevin. Me. Leg.*)

I ran with Hevin at school because we were playing together. (Labels: *Hevin. Me.*)

Then when we ran we fell. I fell! I fell! We said. (Labels: *Hevin. Me.*)

Helping Writers Tell Their Stories

YOU MAY NOTICE more than a handful of children in your class who love to draw. They would be happy sitting with pencils and markers for much of the school day, creating elaborate scenes on paper. During writing workshop, these students may sometimes become so focused on the intricate details of their pictures that they lose sight of the content they want to convey. You'll notice some who more naturally gravitate to other kinds of writing—drawing fantastical images or listing people or things they like, rather than telling stories from their lives. Within this unit, children will create so many pieces of writing that some of them are sure to be about superheroes or princesses. Part of being independent is making independent choices about what and how to write. We do not want to proscribe joyful exploration. But we do want to make sure children are able to tell their own stories with purpose and power. The following is a conference in which I help a child learn how to tell his story; you may need some conferences like this.

After watching Owen add a row of teeth to the grinning sun he'd drawn on what looked to be a beach scene, I pulled a chair up next to him.

MID-WORKSHOP TEACHING   **Going Back to Reread and Add More Details**

"Writers, stop, look, and listen!" I waited until their eyes were on me. "Earlier, when you were writing teaching books, did you write a little while, decide you were done, and then put your heads on your desks and go to sleep? *No way!* You thought to yourselves, 'When I'm done, I've just begun.' We even made a chart to help us know what to do. Let's look again at our 'When We Are Done, We Have Just Begun' chart. I bet all the things we did when we were writing teaching books will work when we're writing stories, too! Let's read over the things we can do. Hmm, . . . We can add to our pictures! We can add to our words! We can start a new piece! We can reread! You know what else we can do? We can meet with our partners! Because our partners can help us come up with more ideas by asking us questions about our writing. Let's add that to our chart right now! All of these things you did when you were writing your teaching books, you can do again, with your stories. Ask yourself, 'What else might I add to my book?' Maybe there are little details you forgot to include, in either your pictures or your words. So before you decide that your first story is done, reread it and think about what more you could put in."

"Hey, Owen," I said. "What are you working on? How's writing going today?" Giggling with delight at his silly sun, he simply pointed at it and said, "Look!" as if certain that I, too, would be amused.

"Tell me the story you are writing today," I probed.

"Look at the sun. I am making the teeth. Ahhhh."

"That is a goofy sun, Owen," I said and smiled. "What I am dying to know right now, though, is what is actually *happening* in your story. Can you tell me about it please? Like what's happening here?" I asked pointing to some figures in another part of the page.

"Well, I went to the beach, see?"

"Aaaah, the beach. Yes, now I see." At this point I knew it was important for me to name for Owen some fantastic things he had already done as a writer and remind him to continue to do them in the future. Only then could I teach him a new strategy that would help him move forward. "Owen, you're doing such important work by telling this story from your life. I can really tell that you thought about a time that mattered and started to get it onto the page. I can tell because you included details about where you were—the beach! Make sure to do that all the time, because I know you have a lot more stories to tell!"

After giving a heartfelt and specific compliment, I zeroed in on the focus for my teaching. "Now that you're so good at finding an important story to tell and getting details about where the story is happening onto the page, I think you're ready for something new. You see, you and I are a lot alike. When I'm not sure what to do next with my writing, I get tempted to do funny stuff, like put teeth on the sun." Owen looked at me with surprise. "Yep. It's true. So what I do instead is ask myself, 'What happened here in this place?' And then I add my answer right into my work."

Owen looked up at me with a slightly puzzled expression, as if perhaps he *hadn't* quite understood his full responsibility as a writer. "It's true!" I continued. "Today I want to teach you how writers do that: think about what happens in the story and then put what happens into their pictures. Let's see how this works. What if we were writing the fire drill story, and we drew the classroom." I quickly drew some chairs and tables, and a few other things to indicate our classroom. "And what if we stopped here and didn't know what to do next? We could ask, 'What *happened* here in this place?' Right?"

Owen pointed to the chairs and said, "When we heard the bell we stood up and pushed in our chairs. We were trying to do it quickly."

Owen's response told me he was ready to move to his own writing. "Wow! Yes, that did happen. We could add that, but let's not do it now, because you have your own important piece to work on. Try it right now. Look at your picture and ask yourself . . ."

"What happened?" Owen gleefully interrupted. "Well, I was at the beach with my mom and my uncle," Owen said, grabbing a blue marker and carefully outlining the top of the sea.

"Is that you there?" I asked, pointing to the smallest of the figures. "Ask that question again. It's working. I hear you telling me about the story. Quick, ask it again!"

"What happened?" Owen giggled. "I was making a sand castle, and then we found the seal."

"*What?!*" I exclaimed. "You were making a sand castle and you found a seal on the beach? You have to tell me about that!" Setting down his marker for a moment, Owen looked up and said, "He was hurt, I think, and this guy that worked at the beach was trying to help him. He was stinky!" He giggled again, delighted.

"Was he okay?" I asked.

"I think so. He was lifting up his flipper at me!"

Next, I needed to teach Owen to record his additional content. "Owen, you absolutely have got to put that into your story! Before we talked just now, I had no idea about all of that important stuff—the sand castle, the hurt seal, the way he lifted up his flipper at you. You are *so* good at putting details into your pictures," I gestured toward the toothy sun, "and as a writer you can work hard on putting in just the details that show *what's happening in your story*. You have a lot of important parts that you need to get into your writing. You have drawn that you were at the beach. What will you do next?"

"I'm gonna do the seal and the seal guy who was helping," Owen said, drawing a rotund creature near the edge of the water, flippers and all.

At the end of a conference, it's important to name what the child has done as a writer and remind him to do this often in future writing. "That's so important, Owen—asking yourself, 'What happened?' and putting that information into your drawing. Thank goodness you did or else we would never know about the seal! After this, will you always look at your pictures and ask, 'What happened?' and then add the information into your work?"

"Yes, and right now I can't forget to put in my sand castle, too." I watched him draw a few items before turning my attention to another writer.

Admiring the Work of Writers in the Classroom

Point out what some writers have done in their writing: include details, depict a small, important moment, write words, and any other things you admire.

"Writers, will you put your writing into your writing folders? Then come join us, folders in hand, on the rug. I want to share some of the ways you used our precious writing time today.

"Writers, would you all admire what Liam did? Liam, show the class your work." (See Figure 12–2.) "Do you see that Liam put details in his picture? He has himself," I pointed to Liam, "and a flower because he was in a garden, and a sun." I pointed to the sun. "Liam told me his story, and it goes, 'One day I went to the park with my dad. We saw flowers. It was sunny.' Liam, are you going to add your dad? Because I don't see him on the page." Liam nodded.

"Writers, would you admire Mikey's work too? Mikey, hold up your story." (See Figure 12–3.) "Mikey has written some words (do you see them?), and they say, 'Me (and my) mom (were) fixing . . .' and soon he's going to tell us what they

FIG. 12–2   Liam's writing

FIG. 12–3   Mikey's writing: *Me and my mom were fixing . . .*

were fixing. The lines in the story are rain because Mikey and his mom were sitting under the trees (see that in the picture?), and it started to rain!

"Matthew did something very special." (See Figure 12–4.) "He made his brother (see, it says *B* for brother), and he decided to make his brother talking. Have you ever seen, in comic books, how they have speech bubbles, and each bubble contains the words someone says? That's just what Matthew did. His brother is saying, 'Want to go to the beach?' And I bet tomorrow, Matthew will tell us what he answers."

"Emma wrote a story that has two pages. She put a picture of a mommy duck here, and a baby duck, and wrote words that went with the pictures. She wrote this." (See Figure 12–5.) "I can't wait to learn what happens next, can you?"

Encourage children to make a plan for how they might try one or more of these things in their own writing.

"Writers, take out the piece you were working on today and hold it in the air. Hold it up high, like a flag, so that everyone can see what you've done.

"Hands down, everyone. Now look at your piece and think about your work for tomorrow. Will you do what Liam, Mikey, Matthew, or Emma did? Or are you getting another idea of how to add to your story? Thumbs up if you have a plan for tomorrow. Wow! That's a lot of thumbs! Remember that idea, and tomorrow you'll be able to get right to work!"

End the writing workshop time with an exclamation of excitement for the writing to come and the start the children have made.

"Wow, look at all you've done! I'm so excited and interested to see what you all will choose to write about next!"

FIG. 12–5   Emma's writing: *I am watching a mom duck and a baby duck.*

FIG. 12–4   Matthew's writing: *"Want to go to the beach*?"

I am going to feed the ducks.

Planning Stories Page by Page

Planning and Telling Stories across Pages

IN THIS SESSION, you'll teach students that writers plan how their stories will go by touching each page as they tell their story.

GETTING READY

✓ Sample of writing with the entire story written on the first page and the rest of the booklet empty (see Connection)

✓ *Creak! Said the Bed* or another simple story (see Teaching)

✓ Summary of *Creak! Said the Bed* or another simple story, written out on chart paper (see Teaching)

✓ A story about something that happened to you, which you will plan across pages, and a blank booklet to model this (see Teaching)

✓ Empty booklets for each student to plan along (see Teaching)

✓ A story about something that happened to the whole class (see Active Engagement)

✓ A completed story booklet that tells more than one story (see Mid-Workshop Teaching)

✓ Single sheets of writing paper and mini staplers in the writing center (see Share)

T HE IDEA FOR THIS MINILESSON came from conferences with individual children. Chances are you have some writers whose stories read as if they are lists rather than stories. Such a writer might begin by writing, "This is my cat. This is my cat's toy." Or, "My cat plays. My cat runs," rather than using story language to write something that sounds more like this: "One day, my cat and I played with a little ball."

To teach these children well, you will want to be sure to buttress your writing workshop with lots of read-aloud time and that the read-aloud time is participatory, with children chiming in to finish sentences you begin. You'll want to be sure that writing workshop is rich in opportunities to tell and retell stories. You'll say to writers, "Can you tell that story once more, really making me feel just how scared you were at that scary part?"

You'll also want to make sure that storytelling precedes children's writing. That is, while it will be important for partners to tell each other the stories they plan to write later, during writing time, it will also be important for children to understand that just before they write a book, it helps to touch each page, in sequence, while saying aloud the story they intend to write. Encourage children to "touch and tell" at the start of every story book, as they have been doing at the start of their All-about books. Encourage them to draw the picture that belongs on a page while thinking about the words they will write to accompany that picture. This storytelling will serve as a powerful form of writing rehearsal. It will encourage children to envision their stories and let the story unfold in small increments.

Today's lesson will teach children they can approach a new piece of writing by planning to write it as a book in which the story is carried across multiple pages.

Planning Stories Page by Page

Planning and Telling Stories across Pages

CONNECTION

Tell writers that today they'll go from writing one-page stories to writing story books or story scrolls.

"Writers, look at this piece of writing. I think the writer might have forgotten something that *this* class knows is really important. Think we could help this writer?" I held up a booklet and turned to the first page. On it were drawings, labels, and sentences. I read the story aloud.

"'One day my sister and I went for a bike ride and then I fell off. I skinned my knee. I was crying and my sister said, 'Don't worry, I'll get Mom.' Mom and my sister came back with a first aid kit. Mom cleaned my knee and gave me a band aid. We all walked home together.'"

I turned to the second page and held it up for the kids to see. It was blank. I turned to the third page and held it up. It, too, was blank.

"Oops! What do you see that the writer forgot? What could we tell the writer to do? Turn and tell your partner quickly!"

I called on a child to share.

"She forgot the pictures and words on the *other* pages!" Annie called out.

"Do you all agree?"

The kids nodded.

"You are right! This story is all scrunched up on one page. The writer forgot to *turn the page*. You all know that when you are telling your stories, you gotta tell each part on a new page of a booklet, so that the story goes across the pages and fills up the book.

"I'm thinking you're ready to learn a trick writers have for figuring out and planning their stories even *before* they start writing."

◆ COACHING

How children thrive on the simple fact that you refer to them as writers and ask for their informed opinions about writing!

✤ **Name the teaching point.**

"Today I want to teach you that, just as writers plan how *information* books will go, writers also plan how *stories* will go. Writers of story books plan from the start how the whole book will go. They touch each page as they tell their story. Then they *turn the page* to say the next thing that will happen."

TEACHING

Point out that a picture book doesn't have a summary, but instead has a detailed story that spans pages.

"Yesterday, I read aloud Phyllis Root's book, *Creak! Said the Bed*. Phyllis could have written her story on one piece of paper." I showed a summary of the book on chart paper and read aloud:

> One by one, all the kids get into bed with their parents, and then the bed breaks.

"But Phyllis knows that a good story builds up slowwwwly. So she decided to write her story as a whole book." I held up *Creak! Said the Bed* and leafed through the pages so that kids would get a feel for the span of it.

"On this page," I opened to the first page, "the parents are snoozing in bed and *then*," I turned the page, "on the *next* page, frightened little Evie enters their room and asks if she can get into bed with them. Momma says, 'Sure!' and Evie *bounces* into their bed! And then," I turned to the next page, "on the *next* page, her sister Ivy shows up, freezing cold. She wants in too. Momma says, 'Sure!' and Ivy *plops* into the bed.

"I bet before she sat down to write this book, Phyllis said to herself, 'Hmm, . . . I need a plan for my book. I gotta get in the mama and papa snoozing and then each of the kids coming into their room, one by one, and the dog too.'

"And so she took out a booklet with enough pages for all those things to happen, and then she told herself her story, turning to a new page each time she told a new part."

Demonstrate how to plan a story across the pages by deciding what will go on each page. Recruit children to help remind you to turn the pages for each new part.

"Let's see if I can do the same. Will you all help me plan and tell my story across the pages? You each have a booklet in your hands. Each time I tell a new part of my story, let's *turn the page*."

I took out my own booklet to model and said, "This story will be about the day I got my cat, Frida. Here I go, everyone. I'm going to tell the first part on the first page. I hope I remember to turn the page when I get to the next part. If I don't, will you remind me?" The kids nodded.

"One day, I went to the shelter to find a kitten to adopt. There were lots of kittens to see in the cages." I looked at the class and everyone tapped the first page.

"I looked—" I stopped and said, "Oops! I forgot to . . . turn the page!" I whispered with an embarrassed look. "Do it with me."

The kids and I all turned to the second page in our booklets.

"Now let me say what happened next. I looked at the kittens inside the cage and I saw a little one make a big yawn! She said, 'Mowwwwwwwwww.'" The kids giggled.

"Wait, I'm going to tell you the best part of what happened next. So what do we need to do?"

"*Turn the page!*" the kids shouted out in unison.

"Oh! It's the last page of my booklet! Here I go!" I turned to the third page and said, "I asked the manager if I could hold her. The manager put the kitten in my arms. She snuggled into my elbow. Her nose was wet. I decided to take her home. The end!"

"Thank you, partners, for helping me remember to turn the page! See how tapping and turning the pages helped me remember each different part of my story? I couldn't squeeze that whole story onto one page! Now I'm ready to draw and write my ideas on each page."

ACTIVE ENGAGEMENT

Remind children of an experience the class has had, and offer a too-short summary.

"Let's say you wanted to write a book about when Mr. Kolk, the librarian, came and showed us three great new books. Would page one be 'Mr. Kolk told us about three books, and then he left. It was fun.'?"

"Nooo," shouted the children.

Ask the children to work with partners to tell the story across pages of a booklet.

"Partner 1, take out your booklet. Partner 2, stay sitting on yours. Work together to tell how the story could go across the pages of the booklet. Partner 2, help your partner remember to . . . *turn the page!*

"One day Mr. Kolk came to our classroom and he . . .' Go!"

The carpet erupted into enthusiastic storytelling and page turning. I listened in, trying to capture snippets of their stories and take note of any students having difficulty.

Even the choice to have my cat say "mowwww" rather than "meow" is meant to teach. Writers try to represent exactly what they want to convey and they don't rely on clichés or other people's words. Sometimes small teaching choices can mean a lot, even when we don't choose to emphasize them to children.

Share an example with the class.

"I heard Gabriela say, 'One day Mr. Kolk knocked on the door. We said, "Come in."' And then she turned the page and said, 'He shared three books with us.' Then she turned the page again, and said, 'And then we all clapped for him.' That is what happened!

"So many of you did what Phyllis does in *Creak! Said the Door*. She doesn't start her story saying, 'The kids all got into their parents' bed.' She starts it: 'One dark night in the middle of the night, Momma and Poppa were snoozing in bed. SQUEAK, went the door.' And then, when we turn the page, the next part of the story is there!"

LINK

Ask the children to take what they have learned here into their writing lives. In this case, they may choose to write a story that goes across several pages of their booklets.

"So, writers, if you are starting a new story today, you might want to try starting with a booklet. Here is a chart that can help you remember how to write a story. Let's read what I've put on the chart so far.

"Practice telling your story by touching each page and saying aloud what happens in that one part, just like you did just now. Then say to your partner, 'Can I show you how my book might go?' And again, touch each page and say what you'll write on that page. You are writing a story like Phyllis Root's story and like mine. This is something you can do from now on: plan! Let's watch the kids at the red table as they get started doing this.

"Remember, remind partners to *turn the page* if they forget! This will help you remember all the things you want to say as you plan your stories."

Five children stood and headed back to their tables where they had already laid out their work. Two sat and started flipping through their new booklets. The others tucked their new booklets into their folders and got to work on their existing pieces.

As you send some children off, help those remaining on the rug notice the good work their classmates are doing as they get started.

"Oh, look! Ryan has a brand new empty booklet. Let's watch and see if he thinks up his story and then touches each page as he says it aloud." I spoke loudly enough that Ryan, of course, followed instructions perfectly, as did all the other children. "Look, he's doing it! Let's watch the kids at the green table, then, and see if they do this too."

Although you aren't telling children to focus on using details, by asking them to spread the same story over more pages, you are asking them to go into more depth than they would normally—in essence, asking them to write with more detail. It's important that you don't give children the impression that you are asking only and exclusively for longer stories.

FIG. 13–1 Beginning of "How to Write a True Story" chart

Helping Students Stretch Their Stories across Multiple Pages

B Y NOW, you will have realized that the hardest part of teaching writing is not leading effective minilessons, but conferring and leading small-group work. The challenge, of course, is that every day, every moment, is new. Children say—and do—the darndest things. This means you are always leaning forward, always expecting the unexpected. It is tempting, therefore, to think that a teacher enters the conferring and small-group section of a writing workshop without any plans, ready to capitalize on teachable moments.

But the truth is, to see all that is happening in the classroom, to read the signals, and to respond in ways that are powerful enough to actually affect what children do, it is very helpful to plan for this aspect of your teaching. Many teachers think through a day's minilesson to anticipate whether most of their conferring and small-group work this day will be in response to the minilesson or whether it will instead help children recall and draw on their full repertoire of learning thus far.

Imagine you decided to use conferences and small groups on a given day to insure that day's instruction reaches all your children. You might start by moving quickly among the class, noting children who seem to be touching the pages of their blank books and whispering their stories to themselves. These children will be well on the way toward employing all that you have taught today, and with a little support you can help them go far. You might carry the book that you used in your minilesson with you and celebrate what you see children doing by saying, "You are doing just like a published author! I remember how Phyllis Root didn't just say, 'We all got into bed together.' Instead, she stretched out that one moment. First, one person came creaking into the room and jumped into the bed. Then, creak, another person came into the room. You did the same thing here. You said, 'It started to rain. Then it rained a lot.' You might even stretch that out more. Like in this page, you could feel one drop of rain. And then . . ."

MID-WORKSHOP TEACHING   **Noticing and Separating Pages that Don't Work Together**

"Sometimes writers get so enthusiastic that they end up writing lots of little stories across one booklet. It happened to me the other day! I was writing a story about a book fair, and then I started writing about the time I visited my grandmother in the hospital and read to her." I held up my book to show them. "You know what happened next? I did it again! On this page, I started writing *another* story about when the librarian introduced me to a new series that I loved, and, uh-oh! all of a sudden, I realized that even though all of these stories were about *books*, they were not a single story. Turns out I had written *three* stories in one book.

"How many of you think that maybe, just maybe, this might have happened to you? That's great! 'Cause it means you have even more stories you can write. When you pause to make sure all your pages really go together—that they all tell about just one story—if you discover that they don't, you carefully rip out the pages that belong to a different story and file those in your folder for another day." I held up my book to demonstrate this. "I'm going to do it now with this book. Watch how carefully I tear the pages apart, right here next to the staples. See? There's only a tiny corner torn off, but the rest of the page can become part of a whole new book!

"Everyone, right now, quickly look over your pages to be sure they go together. One thing that can help is making a title that tells what your story is about, like 'The Time I Went to the Library' or 'Visiting Grandma.' Some of you may want to give your stories a title today."

(continues)

"Don't forget, tell your story to your neighbor at the table. Touch each page and tell what happened. Then *turn the page*."

"Reread your story and make sure you have pictures and words on each page."

"Give yourself a challenge. If you can write a three-page story quickly, think about what new challenge you can give yourself! You might try to add more words in your story or write a longer story."

"If you got started with one page instead of using a booklet, and you need to add more to your story, get more paper! You can tape it on to make a scroll or staple it on to make a book."

"If you are starting a new story and can't think of an idea, remember, think about something that you did! Maybe it will be about something you did that you do every day! Maybe it will be something that you did with a special friend or family member! Think of your idea and get your materials! Don't forget to touch each page as you tell the story."

Of course, in that instance you did the judging, finding ways the child's work was like the text you'd used as a mentor during the minilessons. You can also recruit children to think about whether they have done the things you highlighted.

Meanwhile, there will be some children in your class whose attention seems to be on subjects very far from the one you tried to teach today. For example, when I watched Joseline work, she was alternately adding color to her piece and examining an elbow scab left over from her weekend at the park.

When I asked her how her writing was going, she turned her tiny face toward me. "Oh," she said nonchalantly, "I'm just doing my writing now. Look at what happened to me when I was walking on the log in the park with Gabriela!"

I turned to look at the drawing, expecting Joseline to be referencing the text, but then noticed her scrunching up her sleeve so I could see her wound. I acknowledged the

scrape and the adventure, suggesting she might remember it for another day's writing, and then asked her about her piece.

"It's about when I went the library with my mom. I got to pick out a book by myself to read with my mom." The picture showed a grinning figure near a doorway and a bookshelf that appeared to take up much of the room. Joseline had labeled *chair*, *shelf*, *book*, *me*, *mom*, and *door* (see Figure 13–2).

For a moment, I wasn't sure what I could celebrate, as Joseline had not told me a story, but then I said, "Joseline, I love the way you didn't write *all about* your mom but instead you zoomed in on one moment—when she read to you! Just like Phyllis Root: she didn't write about the whole day, she wrote about one part of the day."

Then I pressed on. "I think that today you're ready to take another step. Because when writers like Phyllis Root have a great story, they write a whole book about it, telling what happens first, then next, and then next. Can I teach you how to do that now?"

When Joseline agreed, I went on to explain that in her story about choosing a book, she had already shown what happens first. Could she add another page to show what happens after that? Soon she was working on stretching out her story across pages.

FIG. 13–2 Joseline's writing: *My mom and I read books in the library. I got a book off the shelf.* (Labels: *Shelf, Door, Mom, Me. Chair.*)

We read together in a big chair. (Labels: *Reading.*)

Planning Pages across Our Fingers

Highlight a child who told his story across fingers and realized he needed more than three pages.

"Writers, I want to congratulate you. You're filling booklets with such amazing stories. They are whole books just like *Creak! Said the Bed*, and like all these books that are on our shelves." I gestured to our library. "I want to share something that Liam did earlier because I think it may help some of you as you continue planning your books. Liam realized that *another* way he could plan his book was to tell the things that happen across his fingers. Liam, can you show us how you told your story across your fingers right now, just like you did before?"

Liam spread the fingers of one hand, and started to tell his story. "I was waiting in the dentist's office. My mom was with me," he said, holding his thumb. He moved to the index finger and said, "Dr. Mindy came in and looked in my mouth." Holding the next finger, he continued, "She put some stuff on my teeth with a buzzy thing." Finally, on the fourth finger, he concluded, "She let me pick a new toothbrush. It had SpongeBob."

"Do you know what Liam discovered while he was telling his story across his fingers? He realized that he had *four* pages he wanted to tell, but in our writing center there are only three-page booklets. Isn't that something else? He had to staple his own booklet together. See?" I held it up. "And even though it has four pages, it's still all about his trip to the dentist's office. It's still all one story. Bravo, Liam!"

Let children know they can make the booklet their story calls for.

"Well, that got me thinking that some of you may want to make *your* own booklets instead of just picking up one of the prestapled ones. But remember that Liam didn't just go grab four pages. He knew he needed that many because he planned his story across his fingers! If you tell your stories across your fingers, you'll know how many pages you need. Some of you will need four pages, too. You might need to make a booklet like Liam did. There are staplers in the writing center."

Some students may come to you asking for more paper or telling you that their stories go across more than three pages. You'll want to coach them to tell their stories across their fingers. They may, indeed, be able to manage a longer story, and teaching them to plan with their fingers will nudge them a little closer to independence.

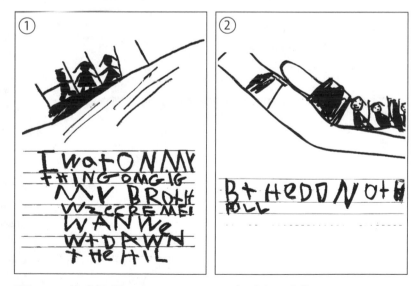

FIG. 13–3   Zoe's writing: *I went on my thingamajig. My brother was screaming when we went down the hill.*

But he did not fall.

Adding More Details to Pictures and Stories

IN THIS SESSION, you'll teach students that writers add details to their writing by thinking about where they were, who they were with, and what they were doing in their story.

GETTING READY

✔ Writing sample from a child whose picture did not capture the details of his or her story as well as the revised version (see Connection)

✔ A story from your own life, a blank booklet, and an idea of how to make a detailed drawing of that story (at least the first page), including where you were, who was with you, and what you were doing (see Teaching)

✔ White board and marker for each set of partners (see Active Engagement)

✔ "How to Write a True Story" chart (see Link)

AS THE DAYS UNROLL, the process of writing will become as much a pleasant routine as snack time or recess. You'll see children taking hold of blank booklets, thinking about the true stories they will write, and then touching the pages of the blank books, saying aloud the words that will go on each page. Most often, children will either draw or sketch a picture on each page before returning to write something down. The act of sketching will help children see and express what they have in their minds, capturing the minute details of a moment on the page.

Once children are progressing with independence, writing and labeling to their hearts' content, you can help them add more to their stories. You'll teach kids that before they put their writing on the "done" side of their folders, they need to think again about the moment and remember all the important parts of the story. They might ask, "Did I write enough information that my readers feel like they are right in the story with me?" and then add details to their pictures and words relating to actions, characters, and setting.

The instruction we often give students to "add details" can baffle young writers. There are many kinds of details, and not all of them are necessarily desirable. This session offers multiple opportunities to learn some specific ways to add details. The minilesson starts off with an example and a "nonexample." This gives students an opportunity to contrast the feeling of having details to that of not having details, as well as helping draw out the purposes for writing with detail. Next, in the demonstration, you'll think aloud not only about the content of what you are adding, but also the process by which you decide what details to add. This is important because the goal is to teach children not simply to add details, but to do so with purpose and intention. Finally, in the active engagement, children will try the process of adding details to the fire drill story or any other shared experience you may have chosen. In the end, you'll aim to give children multiple opportunities to see, feel, and experience the importance of today's teaching.

Today, you'll help children create a world for their story, writing in a way that invites others into their lives.

Adding More Details to Pictures and Stories

CONNECTION

Share the work of one child whose sparse pictures did not fulfill the promise of his wonderfully detailed oral story.

"Yesterday, Matthew told me a story about something that happened with his baby sister. He said that he was eating breakfast at the kitchen table and his baby sister was in her high chair eating dry cereal. All of a sudden, she threw her cereal at him and he started laughing. Then, when his mom came into the kitchen, she started laughing, too. And you know what is so cool about Matthew's story? When he was telling it, I felt like I was right there with him. Don't you feel that way? You could picture it, right? It's because he told really important parts of the story, like where he was and who he was with and what he was doing.

"So then, when I asked Matthew, 'What are you going to draw and write?' He said, 'Me and my sister.' And when I asked, 'What will you write?' He said, 'This is me and my sister.' Hmm, . . .

"Writers, it looked something like this." I held up a booklet with two featureless figures and the sentence, "This is me and my sister." "Writers, can you see the cereal bits in the picture? Do you see the kitchen in the picture? Do you see Matthew's mom laughing in the picture?" The kids shook their heads, no. "Isn't that sad? We all enjoyed Matthew's story so much when he told it, but the story we loved didn't make it onto the paper!"

Show how the child noticed and solved his problem by adding characters, action, and setting.

"Luckily, Matthew realized the same thing. He could tell that what he was going to draw and write on his page didn't match the great story that he had told out loud. He said it looked like he had 'floating people.' I agreed. Well, just look at what Matthew's work looks like now." I held up the new version, full of details that oriented the reader. "You can see the kitchen and the windows, the table, and the cereal and his baby sister and mom! Phew! Matthew knew that his readers needed to know where he was, who was with him, and what they were doing.

"Writers, we have all been working on telling true stories from our lives across pages in our booklets and then drawing and writing those stories. One thing I noticed is that many of you tell these great stories out loud to your partner, but then, when it is time to put them on paper in the booklets, your pictures and words don't match what you said out loud.

◆ COACHING

Teachers, if there is no handy example, you can use your own writing or even use Matthew's! Chances are, though, that someone in your class will have told a detailed story and yet written a generic text and/or drawn a generic picture.

Sometimes they look more like this one, with floating people." I pulled out my featureless figures drawing. "I think we can all learn from Matthew right now."

❖ Name the teaching point.

"Today I want to teach you that when writers write stories, they try to write them in such a way that readers feel like they are right there with them. To do this, they think about where they were, who they were with, and what they were doing on each page, and then they put those details into the pictures and words."

TEACHING

Begin a story from your life as you draw only the sparse details onto a page of a blank booklet.

"Watch me as I try to tell my story and then put it down on the paper so you can feel like you were right there with me—so you can picture what is *happening* in the story. I am going to use our chart to help me remember what to draw and write. (Point to the "How to Write a True Story chart, Figure 14–2, on p. 110.) This will help me remember to write and draw who was there, where we were, and what happened." Last night, I was having dinner with my friend and my cat, Frida, curled up on my feet." As I spoke I drew a stick figure labeled "me" and a circle labeled "cat." I held it up for children to see.

"Wait a minute. Do I have a floating person and even a floating *cat*? Is this another time when the story didn't really make it onto the paper?"

The class nodded.

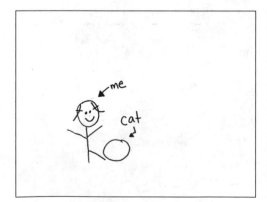

FIG. 14–1   *My writing. Labels: Me. Cat.*

Second version, with additional details: the kitchen table, friend Eleanor, and cat curled at feet.

Last page, with many more details added.

"Uh-oh. Okay, I am going to tell my story out loud, and as I do that, I'll try to fill the page with more details that show where I am, who I am with, and what is happening. Ready?"

Begin the same story, including *who*, *what*, and *where*, and draw these details as you talk.

"First, I'll picture it in my mind. We learned to do that, so I should do it now. So where was I? Oh yes, in the kitchen, sitting at the table. Alright, I'm going to draw the kitchen table right in front of me." I sketched a rectangle and continued to sketch as I spoke.

"Hmm, . . . Who was I with? I was sitting with my friend Eleanor, and Frida was curled up in a ball at my feet, on the floor. Okay, I'm going to draw Eleanor in a chair at one end of the table. I totally forgot her! I was at the other end. What were we doing? Eleanor and I were eating spaghetti and meatballs, and Frida was purring at my feet. Wait, where is the spaghetti? I gotta add it in. And I'll make an arrow from Frida's eyes to show you she was looking at her mouse toy across the room. Oh, I'd better add the toy, too.

"There! Now listen to how my story could sound. The first page will probably go like this: 'One night,' Wait! I can add the moon to show night time out the window! 'One night, Eleanor and I were eating spaghetti and meatballs for dinner. Frida came in and curled up at my feet. I leaned down to pet her. "What are you looking at, Frida?" I said.'

"Can all of you picture that in your mind? Do you feel like you were there with me?

"Writers, do you see how you can picture my story in your mind as if you were there with me? That's because I made sure to tell the important parts of my story, and to also put them on the page—parts like where I was and who I was with and what we were doing. Now that I've done that, I will remember what to write when I get to the words. For right now, I'll add the important labels to my picture." I quickly added a few words. "Now I can turn the page and write the next part of my story!

"You can do the same thing to help you tell and draw and write your stories so that others feel like they were right there with you when it happened."

ACTIVE ENGAGEMENT

Set children up to try the strategy by storytelling a shared class experience with their partners and using white boards to record details.

"Now it's your turn to try. Partner 1, take out your white board. Tell the story about the fire drill with your partner. As you tell the first part, remember to include where we were, who was there, and what we were doing. If you forget what to say, look up at our chart. Then, turn and *tell* your partner just the beginning part of the story." The children turned to face each other and Partner 1's began to tell the story. Some Partner 2's were chiming in with helpful suggestions.

We do this demonstration at a quick pace, so that children don't get bored or lose track of the purpose of this exercise. We hope to also convey to the class that adding details to a drawing is work that writers do quickly to set themselves up for writing.

"Ready? Caps off! Draw and write as many details help show just the first part when we heard the bell ring in the classroom. When you are done, reread your pictures and words and see if you have all the details you need! Go!

"Give your partner help. If she said, 'We stood up and pushed in our chairs,' help her add chairs to her picture and words. And remember, tell *where* we were, *who* was there, and *what* we were doing!" The children drew, wrote, and discussed. After a minute or so I stopped them. "Caps on! Hold up your boards! Oooh, you've done this in lot of different ways, and they all look so interesting. Look around at each other's boards. Notice how even though we're asking the same questions—*where* were we, *who* was there, and *what* was happening—we came up with different ways to draw and write about it."

Debrief by having students picture the details in their minds while one student shares his white board writing.

"Let's listen to Mikey tell the story of the fire drill. Let's see if he has all the information on the board. Go ahead, Mikey, tell the story. If there's something in his story that you can see, put your thumb up on your knee."

"One sunny day—"

"Up! I see something outside the classroom window. The sun!"

"One sunny day we were sitting at our tables."

Thumbs began sprouting up. "Yep. We all see tables!"

We continued in this way for just a little longer.

LINK

Send children off with a reminder to write with details to help readers feel like they are part of the story.

"So, writers, from now on, whenever you are writing stories, you want to help your readers feel like they are right there with you. You can picture your stories in your mind and think about *where* you were, *who* you were with, and *what* you were doing. Be sure to include these details in your drawings and words so that others can feel like they are right there with you, too.

"If you find that you have floating people, or that your story didn't make it to the page, just look back up here at the beginning of my book about Frida. I wrote the word 'Who,' next to the people, I wrote 'Where,' right here next to the things that are in the kitchen, and I wrote 'What is happening?' next to the action in the pictures. This can help remind you to add more details. You can also look up here at our 'How to Write a True Story' chart.

How to write a TRUE story:

* THINK
  · something that happened
  · something you did

* PRACTICE telling with a storyteller's voice

* PICTURES and WORDS tell

who   where   what happened

Reminding Children that Writers Make Time to Write Words

EVEN IN THIS SECOND ROUND of making books, you will probably have students who are still showing beginning-of-the-year tendencies. While most of the class will be willing and able to make quick sketches before moving on to add labels or write simple sentences, other kids will treat each page of a booklet almost as if it exists in isolation rather than being part of a cohesive story. These children might belabor a single drawing (not sketch) with no visible plan for how the pages that follow will build on the first. They may not even have written a single word.

Interestingly, children who fall into this category may not recognize that they are missing the mark. In fact, when you confer with them, they may be able to *tell* the story they are hoping to record, even though what's on the paper doesn't reflect this. Acknowledge the fact that these children have story ideas and plans before gently reminding them how writers make time to draw *and* write the words every day.

When I pulled up alongside Hevin, he had drawn a picture of two figures on his first page, and he was now adding details—a net and a ball, the lights, some benches maybe. It looked like he was settling in for a long session of drawing (see Figure 14–2).

"So, Hevin, what are you working on as a writer today?"

MID-WORKSHOP TEACHING   Drawing and Writing to Show Action

"Writers, one of the ways we talked about adding details today was to think about what people are doing in the story. Well, some of us know exactly how to *tell* what people are doing in their stories but are having a hard time *showing* the action. I was thinking that if we can study what people's bodies look like when they move, we can draw or write in ways that show that movement. If I want to make myself jumping up, I can think to myself, 'What does that look like? What does my whole body do?' I am going to jump up right now. Watch to see what my body does so you can help me draw and write it." I jumped up and threw my arms in the air. "What did you see my body do?"

"You jumped," they reported. I wanted them to notice and name, more specifically, parts of the action that would help them draw or write it, so I focused my questions on parts of my body.

"And my legs?"

"They bent and went up."

"And my arms?"

"They went up to the ceiling!" Now they were getting the hang of it!

"Right, so I can draw myself jumping off the ground," I said as I started to draw according to their suggestions, "I'll make my legs higher than the floor. Maybe make my 'Mo Willems lines' below my feet! And my arms up to the ceiling.

"I can also write, 'I jumped up and reached to the ceiling!'

"Sometimes acting out your story a little helps you find the action to write and draw. Look at your work to see if it makes sense to try this. Show your neighbor the action. See if you can give each other a tip of what to add by watching your actions. Go!"

(continues)

"Don't forget to tell us where you are and show us what is around you. What details can you include so readers can tell where you are?"

"I just saw the coolest thing! Tanisa was about to put her writing away in her folder, but then, you know what I saw her do? I saw her reread her story. She read it to see if every page had enough information, and when she realized it did, *then* she put it on the red dot side. Isn't that great? You can reread your writing to make sure it's really done!"

"I just noticed Derrick adding to the picture *and* the words to help tell the important parts of his story!"

"Think about what your writing needs. Do you need to add *who*, *where*, or *what* to the pictures or words? Make a decision and do it!"

Hevin turned his enormous brown eyes up to me. "I'm writing about how I played basketball with my friend." Turning to the still-blank second page, he said, "He threw me the ball. But I lost the game."

"Wow!" I said, looking at the text. "You are lucky to have a friend who throws you the ball. No wonder you are writing about this.

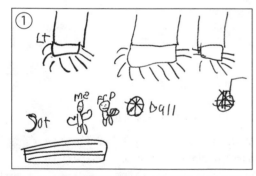

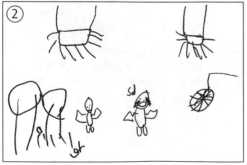

FIG. 14–2   Hevin's writing: *My friend threw me the ball. He shot the ball.* (Labels: *Me. Friend. Ball. Court. Lights.*)

I lost the game and I was sad when we walked home. (Labels: *Sad. Grass.*)

"You are writing a story that matters to you and you know how your story goes. Look, you have planned out all the pages. Such important writing work!"

After a pause, I said, "You know, Hevin, I think you are ready to try what we have been studying about getting pictures and ideas down on the page quickly! You learned that you could draw all your pictures and then write words next to them too. Remember, you don't want to spend the entire time drawing. You need your words, too, to help your reader know who was in your story, what was happening, and where you were."

Hevin nodded vigorously, suddenly holding his lip in, on the verge of tears.

I said gently, "Oh, Hevin, this is a wonderful start to your story! I wouldn't even be wanting the words so badly if it weren't! In fact, I want to read your story so much that I want to help you draw it quickly on the page so that you have time to add words, also. Let's try it now. I'll teach you. The key is to draw whatever you need to tell the story, then add the words. *Then* you can go back in with color and more details."

Looking at the first page I said, "Now, you already have lots of pictures here but no words. Let's try and add some words. We don't need more pictures to tell this part, or colors. We need words to tell us who is here and what is happening!"

"Well, I am on the basketball court with my friend."

"What do you need to label for your readers?"

"Court?"

"I don't know. Are you on the court?" This is vital, so I want to highlight it. I didn't simply respond, "Good, yes, write that down," even though I knew it was a court. I need to build Hevin's confidence to help him become more self-reliant. If I tell him all the things that are good or right, will he be able to carry on without me sitting there? So I put the question back to him, as if to say, "You are the boss of this writing. You get to decide whether it's a court, a park, a playground."

Hevin nodded in answer. "So 'court' would certainly tell us where you are! That's a good idea, then, to include it because it gives the reader information about where you were." I could see that he needed a little more confidence before feeling like he could take this work on independently.

"Where else might you be able to help your readers with a word?"

"Friend? Me?" He asked, again looking up at me for approval.

"It's your story. You get to be the boss and make the decision. What do you think? Will that help the reader?"

"Yes, because that was who was playing."

"Ahh, you remembered the *who* question. I might not have thought of that. So add it in."

Flipping to the last page, which was blank, I added, "Why don't you tell me what happens on this page?"

"Well, I lost the game, and I was sad when we walked home."

I nodded. "Yeah, you must have been sad. Draw that part of the story with just the pen. Draw it quickly. Try to get lots of information about where you were and how you looked and who was there. Then you can go back and add your words." Hevin picked up his pen and sketched himself and his friend and dark lines shooting out of his eyes to show crying. He started to sketch the grass in the park and all of the flowers, but I said, "Remember, you want to add in the words that will help your reader. After you add words you can go back and add more details. Don't forget to make time to write your words, right?" I smiled at him.

"Yeah, I'm done with my drawing, so I can write my words." He then picked up his pencil again and wrote labels next to his sketch. He wrote "sd," and "gr."

I reminded him, "So from now on, remember to do what you did just now: draw your story quickly, write your words, and then add color and details. That way, you always have time for words too!"

Hevin smiled quietly and continued working.

Writing Partners Can Be Writing Teachers

Let children know that partners can offer tips and suggestions to improve one another's stories.

"Writers," I said, "Stop, look, and listen."

"Oh yeah!" the children chanted back.

"Writers, will you hold up the piece of writing you are working on right now? Place that story on top of your folder. Stand up, tuck in your chairs and come to the meeting area with that story.

"You have now spent a few days writing true stories from your lives! You have practiced telling stories to your partner to get a really clear picture of what you want to write. Then, after writing them, you have *read* those stories to each other.

"Some of you have discovered another way partners can be helpful. I have heard some writers in this class give each other tips and suggestions to help make each other's stories even better. Partners can be like little writing teachers to us. They can listen to our stories and tell us what they think our writing needs!

"Partner 1, I am going to ask you to be the writing teacher. I want you to listen to Partner 2's story. As you listen, I want you to think about a few things: does Partner 2 need to add more to the picture or words or tell more about *where* the story takes place or *who* is in the story or *what* is happening? Could Partner 2 add some action? If you think of any tips or suggestions, tell your partner! Of course, it's up to the writer to make any changes, and the writer may not always want to, but it's still helpful for partners to listen carefully and make suggestions!" After a couple of minutes I asked them to switch roles so that everyone would have a chance to both give and receive valuable feedback.

Here, I want to remind children of two important ways they are already being helpful partners to one another, before introducing another.

FIG. 14–3   James's writing: *The time I played soccer with Ori.*

Stretching and Writing Words
Hearing and Recording Sounds in Sequence

$\mathcal{D}$ear Teachers,

In earlier sessions, you encouraged children to stretch out words and record the sounds they hear. Some of your students will have started to listen to sounds in words and to write these sounds down as letters during writing workshop. Others have some knowledge of sounds and letters but are not yet comfortable drawing on that knowledge during writing workshop. Still others may not yet understand the concept of listening for sounds. (One five-year-old wanted to write the word *Santa*. Her teacher said, "Say the word slowly. Ssaannta. Ssaannta. What sounds do you hear?" The child repeated the word again, as if listening hard. "Ssaannta," she said. "I hear 'ho ho ho!'")

Today you will aim to help students develop another strategy for getting words down on paper—listening hard to the sounds in the word, recording those sounds, and then rereading to ensure that they have recorded *all* of the sounds that they heard.

MINILESSON

You will probably choose to remind children of the work they have already been doing as writers to record the sounds they hear to add labels and words to their pieces. Your connection will recall the strategies writers use to hear and record these sounds: saying words slowly to stretch and hear sounds and using the name chart, the alphabet chart, or other classroom tools to find the letters needed to record these sounds. Today you will rally your growing writers to do this and more. You may want to show students the difference between a piece of writing that has labels with one or two letters versus labels that attempt to have a letter for *every* sound.

Reminding children of what they already know gets them ready for today's teaching. You'll recall that a teaching point not only names the larger skill of *what* writers do, but also includes an explicit strategy to explain *how* writers do this work. This language makes your teaching replicable, so children are better able to transfer the strategy to their own writing. A teaching point for this lesson might be, "Today I want to teach you that writers spell words fully so that they can read their stories and so that others can read them as well. One way you can do this is to say the word as slowly as you can, listen closely to the sounds you hear at the beginning, and then write those sounds down. Next, you can say the word again as you reread your writing, this time listening closely for the sounds you hear in the middle, and then again at the end of the word. This helps you write all the sounds you hear in a word, from beginning to end, which will make your writing much easier to read."

Now you'll be ready to demonstrate recording all the sounds of a word in your own writing. Select a page in your story that does not yet have labels. Remind children to watch closely and notice your process, knowing that soon they will have a chance to try it with other words from the page or from the shared text you are creating. To make your demonstration very explicit, you might voice over, or narrate, the steps of your process as you stretch the word, listen, and record each sound. You may also call children's attention to the way you slide your finger underneath the letters you have recorded before adding the next sound. Isolating these micro-details in your demonstration can be the difference between children being able to do it on their own and not being able to. It is helpful to have an enlarged version of your writing on the easel, so that your students can see how you reread and slide your finger across, listening to and recording all parts of the word.

Before moving on to the active engagement portion of the lesson, restate the process you used to record every sound. You might say, "Children, did you notice how I said the word really slowly and wrote down what I heard at the beginning? Then I said the word again and wrote down what I heard next. I even used my finger to slide across the letters I had down on my paper to make sure I put down every sound in the right order. I'm telling you that because you can do the same thing."

This is where you give writers an opportunity to practice this process with another word or text. Perhaps you recruit their help in adding another label to your drawing, or you may have a class book that could use more labels. You might ask the whole class to try the same word, or invite children to choose an object to label from a page of drawings. Either way, you'll remind them to use the same steps to record every sound in order. You can record their suggestions on the chart or give them dry erase markers and a white board to practice this strategy on the rug. Remember that your goal is not to teach children the correct spelling of the word, but rather to coach writers to segment sounds across a word and record all of these sequential sounds in their writing. Use this time to assess their understanding of this strategy and to determine which students need either more support with this work or more of a challenge. This will be useful information for conferring and small-group work. You could "flag" writers with similar needs—giving them a sticky note of a certain color and asking them to hold on to it. Later, you will be able to gather these students for additional practice.

If you want to give children a chance to practice with a little less support before sending them off to work independently, you may decide to ask individual students to say and write a second word and then check it with their partner by sliding their finger under each sound of the word. You can voice over, coaching them to keep saying the word and listening to all of the sounds.

Before sending your children off, remind them of the strategy and invite them to use this process whenever they are writing words, especially those that are hard, because this will help readers be able to read and understand their writing. We often echo the precise language of a teaching point to make these lessons explicit and replicable for young learners.

CONFERRING AND SMALL-GROUP WORK

At this time, you might convene a small group of writers to whom you gave a sticky note during the lesson, supporting them as needed. You will be able to coach this group of students to transfer these strategies into their own work. It might be helpful to have tools, such as name charts and alphabet charts, nearby to offer additional scaffolds.

As you lead individual and table conferences today, your goal will be for writers to add more sounds as they label their drawings and for those sounds to be recorded sequentially. You'll remind children of everything they already know and coach them to use these strategies to tackle trouble. You might do a quick sweep of the room to admire and reinforce expected behaviors, leaning in beside a table and saying, "Can I just stop all the writers at this table for a moment? I am so impressed by the way you are working hard to add more words today! I see James sliding his finger to add more sounds to the middle of his word, and Lindsay has her name chart out to help her find the letters she needs. I hope you are feeling proud of yourselves. You are becoming such strong writers already!"

You may want to pull together a small group for some interactive writing, in which your teaching of letters and sounds is contextualized inside an emphasis on composing a story well. Especially with your newest writers, ones who are still learning their letters and sounds, you don't want to stress stretching out words, hearing all the sounds, or using alphabet charts without also making sure that your students understand the most important things about writing, such as composition and planning. This is where differentiation plays an important role. Your first goal is to ensure that children have lots of ideas about what to write. Then writers put what they can on the page and keep going, trying to say a lot.

You may also pull a small group of students who need to work on hearing and recording sounds in order or who need to get more sounds into their words. When I looked at Draco's piece of writing about going to the park with his scooter, I saw two figures standing on scooters, one of which looked like a little girl. He had three labels: "me," "sun," and "gr." During this small-group session, Draco and the other students worked on recording sounds in order and hearing more sounds in words. Draco also realized he had forgotten to include his dad on the first page of his story and added that as well (see Figure 15–1). The work of small-group instruction is not usually to learn something brand new. Rather, it is designed to provide guided practice and coaching to students so that they can work on internalizing strategies that have been taught to the class.

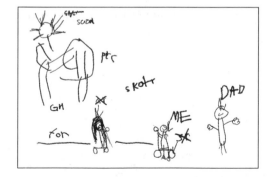

FIG.15–1 Draco's writing: *Me and my dad went to the park. I played on my scooter.* (Labels: *Sun. Girl. Park. Floor. Scooter. Me. Dad.*)

MID-WORKSHOP TEACHING

While students are busy working, you will likely coach them with some mid-workshop voiceovers, challenging them to be brave and to tackle words, even when these seem far too difficult, just like they draw pictures of hard-to-make ideas. "Today I watched Margo. She was writing about art and wanted to say she made an origami bird but she realized that *origami* was a hard word. Do you know what she did? She said, 'Oh well. I'll try it anyway!' Let's all try that word. On a Post-it at your table, try to write *origami*."

You may also want to do voiceovers that reinforce labeling not just things, but actions, or draw students' attention to how many labels they have on one page to the next to make sure they are trying to write many words.

SHARE

The teaching share can reinforce the strategy of the minilesson. You might decide to choose a child to reenact or tell the story of her process of stretching out a long or hard word in order to write it down. You will have talked with the student you have chosen in a conference during independent writing time. That way, the child will have used the words to describe his or her process already. This helps keep share time short and to the point.

You may also want to have every student in the class practice the strategy again. Choose a word from one of your other student's pieces that everyone can write together. Help children feel they can tackle any word in the world they want to write. Allow for approximations, since the point isn't to learn to spell a particular word correctly. You might then choose three more words so that the students get a lot of practice. Acknowledge the differences in spelling in the class to show how students are thinking about sounds in words in different and similar ways. Celebrate these attempts enthusiastically, because they are fundamental stepping stones toward the higher-level work of writers!

Bringing Our Writing to Life
Adding Dialogue with *Speech Bubbles*

HAVE YOU NOTICED that your students can *tell* the most wonderful stories, filled with details, humor, and voice? And have you wondered what happens to these gems in between the telling and the writing? Somehow, the gorgeous stories that surprise and delight you just don't make it to the page. And yet, how could they? Beginning writers simply haven't yet developed the writing skills to reproduce on paper what flows so effortlessly out of their imaginations. Their mouths can tell it faster and more fully than their hands can write it. This is one reason the telling of stories is so important—so youngsters can develop skills orally now that will benefit them as writers soon.

One way young writers can bring their words to life on the page right now is to get the people in their stories talking. Kids understand how speech bubbles work, and a little bit of dialogue can add a lot of animation to their stories. We learn a lot about a mother pointing to a dog when her speech bubble says, "Stop, Fred!" and the dog's says, "Arrrrffff!" The story of a father and daughter in a store is clearer when we read, "Follow me, Grace," and her reply, "I'm going this way."

You may want to teach children to use empty speech bubbles as placeholders at first, using these as cues to add dialogue when they tell their stories. Of course, you probably have a handful of students who, by now, can write simple bits of dialogue, and you will want to encourage these children to go ahead and add any words they can. As with all of your teaching, you'll want to emphasize that speech bubbles are not just for today, or for this story, but also for past and future stories. When they revise for publication in a few days, some writers may opt to add dialogue as part of their revision process. As they add dialogue to today's story, we want them thinking, "I could do this in other stories, too!"

Many teachers incorporate a little playacting, using their hands as puppets, or actual puppets, to model getting their characters up and talking. Kids will love watching your stories come alive! It won't be long before your classroom is buzzing with the voices of all your students' friends, family, and even pets. In this session, you'll teach kids that dialogue invites readers into a story, allowing them to experience it firsthand.

IN THIS SESSION, you'll teach students that writers bring their stories to life by making their characters talk.

GETTING READY

✔ Puppets of well-known characters from your drama center. If you don't have already-made puppets, photocopy images of characters in a book that your kids know well (a villain-hero duo works particularly well), cut out the shapes, and glue them to popsicle sticks. Or prepare to use your hands! (see Connection)

✔ One of your stories that doesn't yet have dialogue, with room for large speech bubbles. Be prepared to reenact the story. (see Teaching)

✔ Writing that students are currently working on (see Active Engagement)

✔ "How to Write a True Story" chart (see Mid-Workshop Teaching)

Bringing Our Writing to Life
Adding Dialogue with Speech Bubbles

CONNECTION

Use puppets to playact a short scene in which two characters speak. Then ask children to take on one role, responding with imagined next words.

"Writers, take out one story from your red-dot side that you feel is finished. Come to the meeting area and sit on your story.

"Hi there, kindergartners," I said as I held up one of their puppets from the drama center—actually a photocopied picture of the biggest billy goat from one of our *The Three Billy Goats Gruff* books, glued onto a craft stick.

"I am the biggest billy goat!" I said. "Remember me?"

"Yes!" The children called out as they started laughing.

"What's so funny?" I said, feigning surprise, staying in character. "I'm looking for the troll. Have you seen him?"

"No!" they shouted out. They were with me now.

Then I pulled out another puppet from behind my back—the troll. "I'm the troll! What do you want?" I said, in my meanest troll voice.

"I wanted to say sorry for bucking you into the wild river with my horns," I made my billy goat puppet say.

Resuming my role as teacher, I asked the children, "What should the troll say back? Quick, turn and tell your partner!" The class brimmed with laughter and chatter. "Let's hear some trolls," I said, as I began to point to individuals to share.

"I am going to eat you now, big billy goat!" Deleana shouted out gleefully, in a troll voice.

"Hey, you pushed me and got me all wet!" Liam pouted, as the troll.

Using dialogue in writing may seem as though it is a complex skill for such young writers, but it actually isn't that new for young writers. Dialogue is something they are immersed in daily in reading and conversations. Kids act like their parents or pretend to be characters in dramatic play centers. They reread familiar stories with characters who talk. And often kids act out these stories, sometimes during choice time or even at recess or in the block center. You may decide to choose a favorite storybook, maybe even one you have created puppets for in dramatic play centers. You can use such puppets to help illustrate what dialogue is and how it helps bring the characters in a story to life.

Make sure children understand that they need to say the very words the character would speak, not talk about the kinds of things he might say. We are helping them rehearse for writing by imagining exact words.

Debrief by drawing a connection between this and the other things you have taught students to do to bring their stories to life.

"See how it's possible to imagine the voices of your characters and make them talk? When you do that, it makes all of us feel like we are there. Just like you made the billy goat and the troll talk, writers all around the world also make the characters in their books talk. You've all learned some ways to bring your stories to life, like adding details and actions. Today I want to show you *another* way writers bring their stories to life."

❧ Name the teaching point.

"Today I want to teach you that writers make characters talk. You can do this by putting speech bubbles by whoever is talking. When you *tell* the story, the speech bubbles will remind you to include what people said. Later, when you *write* the story, you can write bits of talking in the speech bubbles to get down the exact words that people said."

TEACHING

Model adding speech bubbles and bits of dialogue to one of your own stories.

"Let me show you what I mean. I have a story about the time my nephew and I played in the sprinklers. Watch as I point to the people in my story and think about what they said. Then I'll add speech bubbles right next to their heads. Then later I'll go back and write what they said.

"Here's the part when I threw water on my nephew. Let's see, who spoke first? I think I did." I touched the picture of myself on the page. "I'll draw a quick speech bubble right by my head so I won't forget that I was talking.

"Now let's try it with the other person in my story. Here's my nephew running away from me. Did he talk? Hmm, . . . let me try to remember." I touched the picture of my little nephew and started moving my hand like a puppet. "He said, 'No way! You'll have to catch me!'" I drew a speech bubble near his head. "Now I will remember that he talked here, too! Now when I tell my story, I can tell not only where we were and what we were doing, but also what we actually said! So I have the big speech bubbles, and later I can go back and write in our exact words."

Recap by rereading the whole page, including the dialogue.

"Let's reread this page, now that we've thought about what people were saying! Watch how I move my pencil around the picture to tell the whole story! 'One sunny day, my nephew and I went to the park with the sprinklers! I went into the sprinklers and said, "Oh my! The water feels so cool! Come over here. Closer!"' That's what I said. Now I have to remember that my nephew spoke, too. 'He said, "No way! You'll have to catch me!" And off he ran!'" I turned the page. "I chased him! And what do you think happened next? You guessed it, I shouted to him! So I'll put a speech bubble here, too!"

Debrief by highlighting how speech bubbles reserve a place to write the exact words characters speak.

"Writers, did you see how I pointed to the people in my picture and put a speech bubble next to each character who spoke? That will remind me to go back later to fill in the exact words each person said. That's something writers do to bring their stories to life."

You'll need to make sure you model making large enough speech bubbles to fit in plenty of words later so children will do the same!

ACTIVE ENGAGEMENT

Invite children to tell the story they brought to the meeting area, first to themselves and then with a partner, using puppet hands to act out the dialogue.

"Now it's your turn. Take out the story you brought to the meeting area. Look carefully at the pictures and words to help you remember what happened in the story. I see some of you getting your pointer finger ready to touch the first person in the picture. Great! Now ask yourself, 'Did this person talk at this part? What did he or she say?' Think about it and tell yourself the story." I watched as children quietly retold their stories, making sure they were finding opportunities to make their characters talk.

"Now, Partner 2, tell Partner 1 the first part of your story, and see if you can make the people in your story talk. Remember what they said. Move your hand like a puppet if it helps you." The carpet erupted with lively storytelling, as children gleefully acted out bits of dialogue. After a few moments, I asked them to switch roles so that Partner 1's could get in on the fun.

LINK

Tell children they can add speech bubbles not only to *this* story, but to *any* of their stories.

"You remembered which people talked in your stories and even *exactly* what they said! All of your stories will be so much fun for others to read when the speech bubbles are there! You pointed and asked yourselves, 'Did this person talk at this part?' Just like you can add words, pictures, or pages, now you can also add speech bubbles to show the people who talked in your stories. Some of you may even want to add the *words* themselves. You can certainly do this in the story you are holding, and you can also go back to other stories that you wrote to make the people talk in those stories, too."

Coaching English Language Learners

When conferring and working with English language learners in small groups, it is important to know in what stage of language acquisition the students are working. Identifying this can help you develop some language goals as well as adjust your expectations for the kind of language students will produce and how you might communicate best with each one. When you begin to confer with your students, the first stage is always research. You need to know what your students know about writing and what they need to learn. For many English language learners, this will mean studying their pictures intensely, especially those made by students who are at the beginning stages of language acquisition.

For these students, you want to begin to develop a repertoire of ways of talking together, especially if you do not speak a student's first language. For many of these students, hearing a lot of comprehensible language input, language that is contextualized and easy to understand, will be one of the goals of your conference. In this case you may begin by asking students to read back their writing or drawing. If they say nothing, model to show what you meant by "read back the writing." Modeling also introduces new but common nouns that you see in the picture. Begin by noticing and naming what you see in the student's picture. Then move to asking yes-or-no questions, so students can also have nonverbal responses. For example, you might say, "Fatima, I notice you have a sun," then point to the sun in the picture, and follow up with a yes-or-no question to confirm your suspicions: "Is that the sun?" The student may nod. "I thought so! It was a sunny day! Wow. So you have the sun. I see a tree here. Is this a tree?" Continue in this way. When you get to a part you are not sure about, ask, "Is this your mom or dad?" Asking embedded-answer questions is the next step to pushing students' vocabulary and language. If kids aren't ready for this, you can go back to naming. You are trying to establish rapport with your student to find ways of communicating, and are also creating an opportunity for her to hear English and receive some highly contextualized language input.

For students who are in the later stages of language acquisition, it is important to build their academic language. As you research, make sure that you don't "water down"

MID-WORKSHOP TEACHING
Using Our "How to Write a True Story" Chart

"You know an awful lot of ways to get things done in writing workshop. Let's look again at our 'How to Write a True Story' chart. Now I'm going to add 'Use speech bubbles.' Wow! You might decide that your work needs one of these other things today, but always remember that you can make people talk in your story."

your questions. Try to understand students' intents as writers and to think about how to support what you are learning from them. You may find that they have difficulty being specific in their writing. Even in their oral language, students may use a lot of vague language such as, "It was fun. I had fun over there in that place. I don't know what to call it." Before you launch into giving a learner the specific words, push yourself and the student to do a little more investigation. Find out more about the writer. If he has a hard time elaborating, what are his plans for next steps? What is he using to help himself find more things to say in his writing? Then, as you decide what you will teach, you can tuck in ways that kids can talk and write with more specificity.

Once you decide *what* you are going to teach, you must then figure out *how* you will teach it, so that it is clear and explicit for the learner. One way to make a strategy concrete is to use a piece of your own writing to demonstrate a particular strategy, just like you often do in a minilesson. In some situations, such as coaching a student to story-tell stronger stories, it makes more sense to demonstrate with the child's story. In *Up Close*, a DVD of conferences and small groups with ELLs, Amanda coaches several students to improve their storytelling abilities. One conference on the DVD is with a kindergarten student, Melanie. She is working on telling the story about going to the grocery store with her family. In the conference, Amanda coaches Melanie to tell the story with more details, even using dialogue. She does this by first telling a rich version of Melanie's story so that Melanie can hear how her own story can sound. Then Melanie takes over, retelling her story as Amanda continues to coach her to use dialogue and describe action. She supports Melanie in using all of the pictures on the page to help her add detail to her oral story. After multiple retellings (and revisions) of the story, Melanie tells a richer story than she did on her first attempt. Amanda demonstrates for us the delicate dance of following and leading, releasing support as Melanie gains confidence.

Having an example that is in the zone of your students' proximal development is key. You will want to make sure that even for students in the beginning stages of language acquisition, you provide visual examples for them so that your language is contextualized and more easily understood. So if, for example, you want to teach a student to add more, you might show her a piece of writing that literally has one stick figure and a second page that has the same figure with many more objects and the setting included. Then you could turn to the student and say, "What about yours? Can you add more?" Sometimes students copy, because they aren't yet sure what you are asking them to do. Remember that this is a step in the process for many ELLs. You can work on this concept by showing students multiple examples so that they begin to see that it is a pattern and not just a one-time sort of thing you are asking them to do.

When working with English learners, your work takes on another focus. Now you are teaching and coaching both writing *and* language. Knowing a student's stage of language acquisition will help you determine what students need in a conference. Some will be silently absorbing all the language they hear, while others are bravely saying what's on their minds, taking risks and approximating English syntax, and still others will sound almost fluent, though they are still learning. Allow students' drawings to help ground their language in something concrete and comprehensible to them. They will be able to use the schema of their own experiences to find meaning in what you say to them. This kind of communication is important for all your language learners, but especially those in the earliest stages of language acquisition. Don't worry if they are silent. Trust that they are soaking up what they hear you say. If you are at a loss for what to teach in this part of the unit, try dialogue. I have found that many English learners use this skill quite easily and effectively because they can write it in the present tense and it is applicable to their daily lives.

You may have to remind yourself that you are following the meaning and purposes that students have chosen to pursue in their writing. Sometimes, as teachers, we can't help but notice the best spot to add information or the best way to revise. We determine for the student what is important. It happens to the best of us, this urge to improve the writing rather than teach the writer how to make independent and purposeful decisions for his or her own work. It is critical that we ask what a student thinks is important and then listen to the response. Remember that your role in the conference is not as the decision maker, but as the guide to support students in realizing their vision.

How to Write a True Story

Recruit the children's help to begin a chart about how to write a true story.

"Boys and girls," I crooned, "Your teacher tells me you've been learning how to write stories. Is that right?" As they shouted their agreement, I lowered myself carefully onto the stool and said, "I have always wanted to learn how to write a story. Oh yes, you live this long and you have lots of good stories to tell." I paused. "Do you think you've learned enough to teach me, Grandma, what I need to do to write a story?" The kids nodded. Margay was already up on her knees.

"You tell what people say to each other!" she shrieked.

"Hmm, ..." I scratched my chin. "I could write, 'Hello, kids. Nice to see you.' And that would be my story?"

"You gotta think of something that happened!" Fabian called out.

I continued prompting and calling on kids until we had compiled a chart on writing true stories. Stepping out of the role of Grandma and into the role of teacher, I said, "Super Writers, you have learned so much about storytelling! Right now, take turns sharing your work with your partner and then help each other think about what you will do tomorrow. Give each other any tips or suggestions you think might help. Will you add more words to your story? Do you need speech bubbles? I'm going to pass out some Post-its so that you can mark the parts of your stories where you'll be adding on."

FIG. 16–1 Hailey's writing: *I fell off the ladder. My mom gave me a band aid.* (Labels: *Clouds. The Slide. Mom. Me. Sun.* Speech bubbles: *"Hailey are you okay?" "Yes."*)

I felt better. (Labels: *Cloud. The Slide. Floor. Me. Mom. Sun.* Speech bubble: *"I'm okay."*)

I wanted to invite children to share their learning in a way that felt more purposeful than simply listing strategies, so I invited lovable, silly Grandma back for a lesson in story writing. Hunching my back and holding an imaginary cane, I hobbled to the front of the room as Grandma once again, much to the delight of the class. You may have a different character or puppet to story-tell in these kinds of situations.

Using Everything to Make Pieces the Best They Can Be

IN THIS SESSION, you'll teach students that writers reread their stories, drawing on everything they know to improve them.

GETTING READY

✔ Your writing folder, with a variety of finished and unfinished stories. Be ready to select one to revise in front of the class (see Teaching and Active Engagement).

✔ "How to Write a True Story" chart (see Teaching and Active Engagement)

✔ Personal copies of the Narrative Writing Checklist for kids (see Link)

SOMETIMES, IN WRITING WORKSHOP, our job is not to teach a new strategy, but to help students learn how to orchestrate a repertoire of skills and strategies. In this lesson, we help students reflect on their stories to decide what their writing needs. Just as you helped your young writers reflect on their teaching texts not so long ago, now you will guide them to read their stories with the same eye toward revision.

Today's lesson is taught a little differently from the rest. It is what we call an *inquiry lesson*. Rather than explicitly teaching a single writing strategy, we instead invite children to think critically about what their writing needs. They can refer to the items on the "How to Write a True Story" chart, but are also welcome (even encouraged) to consider alternative ways to revise. What makes it an inquiry lesson is that students *inquire* into a topic alongside the teacher; in this case, "What does my writing need?" Try, also, to welcome suggestions that hadn't occurred to you. Children will have them, and they are a gift.

Children will choose a piece from their own folders and think of how to revise it. They should revise more than one piece before choosing which to publish. Children's stamina for revision and editing this early in the year may be low. They may only add a couple of things to a single piece during this session, so you may need to provide a lot of encouragement to keep at it. Replicating the process in many different pieces in their folders will help your students build stamina as well as internalize what it means to revise.

At the end of the workshop you may want to extend the share time a bit. Invite students to look through all of the writing and revising they did today and choose one special piece that they want to publish and celebrate. Children may continue to work on other pieces in their folders, but this piece will be the first one they pull out each day to fix up and fancy up for publication!

Using Everything to Make Pieces the Best They Can Be

CONNECTION

Make an analogy to help children understand the purpose of preparing their work for publication.

As soon as every writer was seated on the rug, I leaned in with a smile and whispered, "Can I tell you a story?" Eager nods answered me. I continued, "Last weekend, my best friend came to visit me, and I baked cupcakes for her! I wanted to make her the most delicious cupcakes. I wanted them to be the absolute best they could be before I shared them with my friend.

Here, I use a metaphor to capture children's imagination—I'm betting the image of the cupcake will stick with them!

"Before she arrived, I looked back over every cupcake to find the best one. Some were a bit burnt and others weren't very fluffy. Then I found a cupcake that looked pretty delicious! But this cupcake was for my very best friend, and I wanted to make sure it was *extra* good. So, I checked to make sure I remembered to do everything I know how to do when I make cupcakes." I counted across my fingers as I went through my mental list. "I checked that the cake was fluffy. I checked to make sure there was enough frosting. I even checked to make sure I used sprinkles, and when I saw that there were *no* sprinkles on top, I added them right away! I fixed it up so that this would be the best cupcake ever.

"Writers do the same thing before they share their stories. They think, 'How could I make it even better?' How could I fix it up?'

"You are going to want to do the same thing with your stories before sharing them with people you really care about! You aren't going to check to make sure that your stories have sprinkles and frosting, are you? No! That would be silly! You *will* need to check for things that make for a good story, though. Good thing Grandma was here yesterday and we made this chart!" I gestured toward the chart, "How to Write a True Story." (See page 129.)

♣ Name the teaching point.

"Today I want to teach you that writers reread their stories, thinking about what they can do from everything they know about good writing to make their work the best it can be."

TEACHING AND ACTIVE ENGAGEMENT

Demonstrate choosing one text to reread and revise.

"First, I need to pick one story from my folder. I don't want just any old story. Nope, I want one that I really like." I quickly looked over the pieces in my folder and said, "I am going to choose this story, about playing in the sprinkler with my nephew, to work on right now. I love it, and I can see that it could use some more work to be even better! Listen as I read it to you, and then, together, we can search for all the things I did well. Then I'll need you to help me decide what else I can do to fix it up."

Ask children to help you compare one of the stories you wrote during this unit to the chart, "How to Write a True Story," starting with the first page.

"Do you think you can help me do this?" The children let out a unanimous, "Yes!" Some jumped to their knees, eager to get to work.

"Let's read each page carefully, thinking about what I have and what I might add to make this even better." Using my pencil as a pointer, I began to tell the story. I started by pointing to the sun and moved my pencil as I spoke, "'One sunny day my nephew and I went to the park, where there are sprinklers. I went into the sprinkler and I said,'" here I pointed to the speech bubble, "'Come here!'" Then I pointed to the other speech bubble. "He said, 'No way! You'll have to catch me!' And off he ran!"

I turned to the class and said, "Now let's read the labels that I made." Again, I pointed as I spoke. "'The sun.' 'My nephew.' 'Me.' 'The sprinkler.' 'Cool.' I have a few pictures on the page, and lots of labels. So far, so good! Now let's check to see if I have the things that I need for a good story!

"As I point to each thing on our chart, give me a thumbs up, if I have it, or a thumbs down, if I need it. Check in with your partner as we do this."

As I read the chart aloud, pointing to each item, I scanned the class to make sure kids were discussing each item briefly before giving me a thumb signal.

Notice that I began by explaining how I go through all of my writing in search of stories with potential, so that children will do the same. I want them to notice that I'm not necessarily looking for pieces that need more work, but rather for pieces that deserve more work.

How to Write a True Story

- Think of something that happened or that you did.
- Practice telling the story in a storyteller's voice.
- With pictures and words
  - Tell **who** is in the story.
  - Tell **where** the story takes place.
  - Tell **what** is happening.
- Use speech bubbles to show what people said.

The first page was fairly simple, since I had done everything on the list. Now that children had the idea of listening critically, I was ready to solicit their help in revising the rest of my book. "We went through the whole list with thumbs up for everything! We're not done, though. We have to read *all* the pages."

Turn to the second page and ask partners to decide what your story has and could use, prompting and supporting them as needed.

"As I go through the next page, think about our chart and talk about each item with your partner. Get ready to give me a thumb. Here is the page where I was chasing my nephew. There I am and there he is. I have a couple of labels: 'me' and 'my nephew' and 'sprinkler.' This page goes, 'I ran after my nephew.'" As I pointed to my picture and labels, and then told my story, partners whispered with one another and put out evaluative thumbs, up or down depending on their decisions.

"I didn't get as many thumbs up this time, did I? I agree! I guess I could add more into my picture, like, umm . . ." I looked to them for help.

"Tell us *where* you were!" suggested Matthew.

"Oooh. Yes, of course! I am going to add the sun and write 'hot sun.' I am going to add the benches where my sister was sitting and watching us." As I added these things into the picture, I asked, "Where else on the chart did you have your thumbs down?"

"Someone else was there!" Sophie offered.

"Wow! I almost forgot my sister when I drew the bench!" I quickly added her to my picture, asking for help with the labels. "I added to the picture, but what about the words?"

"The benches!"

"My sister!"

"I am going to label both! What else do I need?" I moved my finger down the list. "I see thumbs down about speech bubbles. I don't have any, but I was talking and so was he! I am going to put speech bubbles here and then go back to add the words that we said." I drew the speech bubbles and then turned to the last page of my story.

Ask students to work in partnerships to name what you have on the last page and what you need.

On the last page of my story, I had drawn and labeled three floating figures. "Here is a picture of my sister and me holding my nephew. I wrote the words 'me' and 'my nephew.' This part of the story is supposed to go, 'My sister and I caught my nephew and carried him over to the sprinkler. He was laughing and said, "I want to get wet!" I said, "Get ready to feel cool!"' As I look at it now, I can see that I need a lot of help! So turn to your partner and think about what I should add here. Use the chart to help you decide. Don't just say one thing and then stop. This page needs lots of work!" The children immediately started discussing my sparsely detailed page.

As I listened in, I noticed that many seemed focused on speech bubbles. I wanted to coach them to think about more of what they had learned in the past couple of weeks. I pointed to the chart as they talked. "I heard a few people mention speech bubbles. Think about what else I need. Look at our chart. *Who else* was there? *Where* was I?" This little nudge got them talking about more items from the chart. I noted some of the ideas I heard before stopping them to share.

"Wow! You all found lots of things I could add. I heard speech bubbles, of course. I heard some ways to show where I was, like I could add the sprinklers, the benches, and other things that were in the park. That means more words, too. Someone said I should write, 'My nephew was laughing!' Someone else said I could add those little action lines, like Mo does! Such a great idea, and it's not even on our chart! I can draw a couple of those lines right here next to 'Tell what is happening,' though.

"Thank you for helping me figure out what I needed! When I finish this piece, I can go back to *another* story in my folder and check to see what that story needs. I can reread it and think, what do I have and what do I need to help make the story come alive? I can add to my other pieces, just like I did with this one."

LINK

Remind children of the work that writers do to get their pieces ready to publish. Review the Narrative Writing Checklist with them.

"Super Writers, your folders are brimming full of pieces. Before you start any more new piece, reread your stories to make sure they are as delicious as possible and that you use *everything* you know about writing true stories to help them come alive. Remember to include lots of details in your pictures and words."

I pointed to the chart and said, "The chart can help you find things to add, and you might have an idea that's not even on the chart! I can't wait to see all the ways you can add to your stories." And don't forget that you can *also* look at the checklist.

I revealed an enlarged reproducible version of the Checklist for Narrative Writing (see the online resources). As I'd done earlier in the unit, I read through the checklist with them, discussing any items that might be confusing.

As I sent children off to work, I encouraged them to do this with many pieces from their folders. "Don't just work on *one* story. Try to make *lots* of stories better so that they are ready to share with your partners at the end of workshop!"

Narrative Writing Checklist

	Kindergarten	NOT YET	STARTING TO	YES!	Grade 1	NOT YET	STARTING TO	YES!
	Structure				**Structure**			
Overall	I told, drew, and wrote a whole story.	☐	☐	☐	I wrote about when I did something.	☐	☐	☐
Lead	I had a page that showed what happened first.	☐	☐	☐	I tried to make a beginning for my story.	☐	☐	☐
Transitions	I put my pages in order.	☐	☐	☐	I put my pages in order. I used words such as *and* and *then, so*.	☐	☐	☐
Ending	I had a page that showed what happened last in my story.	☐	☐	☐	I found a way to end my story.	☐	☐	☐
Organization	My story had a page for the beginning, a page for the middle, and a page for the end.	☐	☐	☐	I wrote my story across three or more pages.	☐	☐	☐
	Development				**Development**			
Elaboration	My story indicated who was there, what they did, and how the characters felt.	☐	☐	☐	I put the picture from my mind onto the page. I had details in pictures and words.	☐	☐	☐
Craft	I drew and wrote some details about what happened.	☐	☐	☐	I used labels and words to give details.	☐	☐	☐
	Language Conventions				**Language Conventions**			
Spelling	I could read my writing.	☐	☐	☐	I used all I knew about words and chunks of words (*at, op, it,* etc.) to help me spell.	☐	☐	☐
	I wrote a letter for the sounds I heard.	☐	☐	☐	I spelled all the word wall words right and used the word wall to help me spell other words.	☐	☐	☐
	I used the word wall to help me spell.	☐	☐	☐		☐	☐	☐

Nudging Students Toward Next Steps

EVERY SO OFTEN, it becomes necessary to take your children's work home and sort it into piles based on what writers need or are ready to learn next. Studying their writing and looking for patterns and trends will help you decide more quickly what you want to teach in a conference or small group. Some small groups will need to meet with you only once, while others might require a multiday cycle of brief sessions. In any case, you will want to make sure that these groups feel fluid and manageable and that they tackle the challenges students face. As you study their writing, try not to look only at what your students are *not* doing, but also at what they are *almost* doing. Notice signs of them approximating things that they can't quite do on their own or that they don't do consistently. This will help you identify what the psychologist Lev Vygotsky termed their "zone of proximal development." Our most effective teaching focuses on the concepts children are just on the verge of learning, so it's important to be aware of what young writers are reaching for in their work.

Some students will have heard your encouragement to draw with detail and gone overboard. Their drawings may be so time-consuming that these children are not spending much time on writing. The joy of markers on paper may have enticed some children into decorating every dress and coloring every blade of grass. For others, drawings may be a refuge from writing. Now is a good time to pull these students into a small group. Gently say to them, "You have all become so strong at showing what you need to show in your work. Now you're ready for another important thing writers do. Writers are always asking themselves, 'What do I want to *say*?' You can do the same thing! Look at your picture, study it, and then write what *you* want to say! Let's do that now. You can start while I'm here. I will help you for a bit, and then I will let you continue by yourselves." Some students just need a little liftoff, and the small-group time can provide that support.

Some children will write what seems to be random strings of letters. Catch these children in the act so you can discern if these letters are, in fact, random. A child could say, "I rode my bike to the store. I got bread," and use print somewhat correctly (but incompletely) to record "IRDMB2USRIGTBD." Chances are that such a child will have

forgotten what he or she wrote and that you will conclude erroneously that the child copied any letters he or she saw, all in a row, with no reliance on phonics. The trick is to catch a child in the act of writing so you can understand the logic that informs it.

MID-WORKSHOP TEACHING   Partners as Writing Teachers

"Super Writers, can I have your eyes? Thank you. I was just listening to Yatri talk about her writing. I asked her what else she thought her writing needed. She wasn't sure. But then Owen, who sits right across from her said, 'You need to make people talk!' Yatri and I looked at each other and then we looked down at the page. We both thought, 'That is exactly what this piece needs!' And in a snap, Yatri added a speech bubble! It was like Owen was her teacher!

"So, I am guessing that many of you could benefit from another set of eyes and ears on your pieces, from a quick suggestion of what else you could revise. Right now, with your partner, decide who is going to read first and who is going to teach first." Partners quickly negotiated and then turned back to me for the next step. "Writers, read your writing, holding it so you can both see. Teachers, think about what the writers could add or change. Writers, listen to what the teachers say, and if you agree, add it! Check the chart right here, or even my writing on the easel, if you are not sure what kinds of suggestion to give."

I observed the students, pleased at the seriousness with which they took their roles. When I noticed that some were using their pencils to add, I asked them to switch roles. When all of the writers had tried a couple of suggestions, I set them back to work, giving them the choice to continue where they left off or try some of their partners' tips on other pages or other pieces from their folders.

"Writers, remember, once you get the *who*, the *what*, and the *where* in your picture, be sure to add the words next to them as well. I might not know that picture is your mom or your grandfather or your cousin! Remember, write details with words, too!"

"I see Yatri and Deleana looking at the chart and checking to see what they need! Don't forget to check the chart."

"Don't just add one thing! Check the chart again and see if you can add a few things to your page. Jose found three things to add on just one page! Try it! See if you can add more than one thing to your page! Then turn the page and do the same thing."

Some children are beginning to write sentences, but all the words are mushed together. Strategies that can help children at this stage of development are putting spaces in between words, planning sentences and pointing to the paper as they say the sentence before writing it down, drawing an underline where each word might go, and rereading as they write.

Regardless of whether children are writing labels or full sentences, they might need to work on the same skill in a small group. For instance, some writers might need help with including *who* is in the story or *where* the story takes place. Joseline has added the setting to her piece, using both pictures and labels. Here, she shows when she is in the *sala* (living room in Spanish) and when she is outside getting ready to ride her bike (see Figure 17–1). She reread her writing to make sure all the words were on her paper, added information about setting, and used pictures and words.

Of course, you might need to reinforce your minilesson idea and help students reflect on their pieces in a small group. You may decide to use your mentor text and have students inquire and think about what Phyllis Root used in her story. Then have students go back to their own pieces and name what they have already done and what they have yet to do. Allow them to use a fun tool, such as mini Post-its, to identify places in their drawings or labels that they need either to create or add to, or even places to write sentences. Don't forget to consider ways to help students make decisions about what *they* think their writing needs.

FIG. 17–1 Joseline's writing: *One day I wanted to ride my bike. My bike is in the Sala* (living room). (Labels: *Sala. Me. Bike.*)

I was telling my mom I wanted to ride. My mom was watching TV. (Labels: *Me. TV.*)

Then I went outside with my friends to ride my bike. (Labels: *Me. Outside. Bike.*)

Selecting Pieces for Publication

Show children how to sort their work into two piles: pieces they may want to publish, and pieces they definitely do not want to publish.

"You have been adding so much to your stories!" After complimenting their work, I leaned in a little and spoke in a solemn tone. "A special day is just around the corner. After writers have been writing for a while, they choose a piece that makes them feel proud." I let this concept hang in the air for a beat before continuing. "And they publish it. They share it with the people that matter to them. We are going to do the same thing. We are going to get our writing ready to publish so that we can put it in the library and read it aloud to our friends." A couple of kids put their hands over their open mouths. "I am going to ask you to pick a special story you are absolutely crazy about! Then, you are going to spend a couple of days fixing it up for publication."

Ask students to choose a piece of writing to work on and to publish at the end of the unit.

"Would each of you, right now, make a 'yes' pile and a 'no' pile of your writing? And then, go through your 'yes' pile and choose a piece that you want to fix up and fancy up for publication. Choose one that is so good and so special that it deserves hard work to get it ready to share. We'll work with our selections tomorrow. Put yours right on top of your folder. I will give you a star Post-it to put on top so you remember which one you want to start fixing up tomorrow. The rest of your pieces can now go back into your folder."

Get students ready to pick up tomorrow where they left off today.

I wove my way through the children on the carpet, putting a star-shaped Post-it on each chosen story. With mounting enthusiasm, I made little exclamations about each one. "Ooh, you picked the hamster story! Wow, I can't wait to see what you add to this playground piece! This is so exciting! Now, think for a minute about how you can add to this writing. Whisper to a partner the first thing you are going to add when you work tomorrow."

Soon, children will be used to the fact that we choose a piece to publish near the end of each unit, and they will be able to do so in less time and with more independence. Right now, it is still an event that requires a lot of conversation, a little demonstration, some coaching, and even a hint of specialness. I ended their independent work time earlier than usual so I could have a good fifteen minutes for the teaching share.

When I ask children to choose one piece of writing from the many they have done, I want them to choose the piece that gives them the most pride, that tells the story they most want to share, that inspires them to put effort into revision and editing. The pieces they choose may not be the same ones you would choose. They may not seem that great at all on first glance. Children need not choose stories that are already close to perfection. Rather, they must choose work in which they see the seed of possibility. I may ask them to choose their best work, but what I want them to do is choose the piece with the most potential to become their best work.

Editing

IN THIS SESSION, you'll teach students that writers edit their writing by rereading their words and rewriting them, if necessary, to make their writing more readable to themselves and others.

GETTING READY

✔ Piece of writing about a shared class experience, rewritten across several sheets of chart paper, with several misspellings of common sight words (see Teaching and Active Engagement)

✔ A pointer (see Active Engagement)

✔ Colored pencils for yourself and for each table of students (see Mid-Workshop Teaching)

✔ Narrative Writing Checklist for each set of partners (see Conferring) 👉

✔ Children's writing folders (see Share)

OFTEN, STUDENTS REREAD THEIR WRITING QUICKLY, glancing over their words in a sweep and declaring they are done. In this lesson, you'll teach students to reread carefully, pointing underneath each word. This is valuable for children, even if their spellings are abbreviated and their reading skills emergent. Locating their labels and isolating the words they have written helps kids internalize the concept of a word. Saying each word while sliding a finger underneath the letters helps them practice phonemic awareness and segmenting sounds while also checking to see if they have all the letters they need. Another important outcome of rereading is that children come to see their writing as reading material for an audience. This pushes them to read their work with attention to what the piece needs to make sense.

In today's lesson, you will teach students how to reread, check, and fix their writing. Allow your understanding of spelling development to guide the work in your class. Many kindergarten students at this point in the year have approximated spellings in their labels. Encourage them to check their spelling by trying to write the word again, adding letters they might have forgotten. By trying the word again, they may hear more sounds than in their first attempts. Many teachers let students use white correction tape during editing. Less pricey alternatives are blank address labels or mini sticky notes to cover up their first try and try again. I suggest that children simply cross out their first attempts with a single line and try again right above the word. Either way, convey to your students that writers don't just try one thing. Sometimes they try a couple of times to make their writing more memorable to themselves and more readable to others.

For now, I suggest that fixing up involves adding to the picture and the words, and fancying up means adding a cover or a bit of color. Of course, any child can surprise you by doing more. Children who finish early might spruce up their work with the kinds of details they noticed in published books in the classroom library: dedications, awards, author bios, and so on.

Editing

CONNECTION

Remind students of the process they have gone through up to now to create amazing stories.

"Super Writers, tomorrow is the big day—the day of our celebration! Today is our last chance to work on your writing to get it ready to share with the community! Just like when you finish a puzzle, there are still a couple of pieces left to add in your writing. You just have to figure out how to make the last things fit together perfectly to finish.

"Writers, just in case you don't realize how amazing this is, I'm going to remind you of all you have done so far. You started with teaching books, and they were so impressive. Then you learned about writing true stories from your lives. You practiced telling our stories well, then we wrote our stories and—my goodness—we needed *books!* We learned about adding details so readers would know who is in the story, where they are, and what is happening. You even learned to make your people talk by adding speech bubbles. As writers, you learned how important it is to work with a partner and to reread your work. Sheesh. You are so fancy! Take a look at the writers in this room!"

Now that I had given a full accounting of the amazing distance they had come, I wanted to set them up to travel those last few feet to the finish line—of this unit, that is. "Writers do everything you have already done, and they also do *one more thing* before they are ready to publish their work." I sat quietly for a beat. The children looked at me expectantly, and finally Dimitry blurted out, "What?!"

"Good question! They edit their writing (that's what writers call it). Can you say that word: *edit*? When they edit their writing, writers check everything to make sure people can read it. Writers check their words and try to spell those words the *best* they can so that they can."

❖ **Name the teaching point.**

"Today I am going to teach you all about how writers edit their writing. They sometimes try to spell their words again so that they can remember them and help others read them, too! They reread each word and make sure the word looks right. Then, they may even need to change it to make it more readable."

◆ COACHING

We cannot overemphasize the importance of making today feel momentous. It is! And you will want your young writers to grasp the enormity of the progress they have made—and of this chance to share the results of that work with an audience.

Children will remember more when they are active. Even when they just voice the word, edit, *they are being active. When they are observing a demonstration, they must be actively involved—thinking, deciding, processing, reflecting—anything besides passively watching.*

TEACHING

Edit your own writing in front of the class. Think aloud during your demonstration so the students can see the kinds of strategies you use.

"Watch as I edit our piece about the library. First, I need to reread our writing, making sure the words look right. I better put my finger underneath the words so we can look at each word carefully."

I read aloud until I came to a misspelled word. "Hmm, . . . This word doesn't look right." The word *door* was spelled *dr.* "Let me try to make this word look right." I said the word again slowly, sliding my finger under the label. "Let me see if I hear other sounds that I forgot. Think about what letters I forgot." I continued to say the word slowly, sliding my finger under it. "I forgot the *o!* And I know where the word *door* is!" I pointed to the door, wrote the correct spelling above *dr,* and crossed out *dr.* I continued to read with my finger underneath the words. I stopped one more time, to question whether *library,* spelled *Le,* looked right, and then followed the same process to fix it. "Writers, did you notice what I did to make sure my words looked right?"

"You read it all over again using your finger," Margay said.

"Just like in reading!" Owen called out. "I use my finger in reading."

"Good point, Owen, some of us put a finger underneath the words as we read. Did you notice that I also checked to make sure my words looked right, and, if they didn't, I tried them again? Sometimes you can find the word you want in the room, and sometimes you can say it slowly and hear new sounds. If so, write it again!"

Notice I did not erase my spelling but rather crossed out the word with a single line and wrote above it. This is something that I hope students will do. This allows their changes to be visible and lets me see the kinds of editing changes that they make.

Here, I didn't find lots of words that required work, because I didn't want to demonstrate an editing process that is too ponderous. I also didn't try to tuck lessons about punctuating and spelling high-frequency words into this one. It's tempting, but one thing is enough!

ACTIVE ENGAGEMENT

Invite children to join you in doing the same thing you have just done, using a new text (in this case, another page of the same story).

As I flipped the chart to the next page, I said, "So let's try that again, together, with the next page of our story about the library. I'll put my finger under the words and we can read it together. As I do, think about whether we need more letters. See if each word looks right or if you'd change it. After we have read the whole story, talk to your partner and then I'll ask for your suggestions."

Together, as a class, we read the whole page. I slid the pointer under each word, and we said each one twice: once in a normal reading voice and once

FIG. 18–1 Tanisa's writing: *I was going to the park. I said to my mom, Can I go to the park? And my mom said yes.* (Labels: *Mom. Flower. Me. Building. Sun.*)

And I was really happy. (Labels: *Mom. Me. House. Sun.*)

I was climbing the slide. (Labels: *Sun. Slide. Park.*)

slowly, listening to each sound. Many of the students shouted out suggestions. After we had read everything, the students turned to their partners, telling each other what changes they would make. I listened in so I could highlight certain conversations when we came back as a group.

"Super *editors*, what great ideas you have! Matthew and Zoe, can you tell the rest of us what you noticed?"

Matthew began, "Well, when we were reading that page, we saw the word *book* written next to the picture of one of the books that Mr. Kolk brought us, but it's spelled *bk*. Zoe said that she didn't think that looked right, so we thought we should check in our classroom library to see, and look! That basket over there that says "ABC Books" has *books* spelled with *two O*s! So we need to change *bk* to *book* in our writing!"

"You must feel proud to have solved that problem! Now we'll all remember to look at the words in our room!"

Next, I highlighted students who used a different editing strategy. "Annie and Tanisa, can you share with the other writers in the room what you noticed?"

"It says *truck* (*tk*). When we said the word sloooowly and stretched out the sounds, we heard *another* sound!" Annie was overjoyed to share this.

"You did?" I questioned. "Tell us what you heard."

Tanisa cut in, "We heard a /r/."

"Like *rabbit*! So, we must need an *r*!" I said, pointing toward the alphabet chart in our meeting area.

Owen quickly chimed in, "I heard an /uh/ sound, like *umbrella*. And that's a *u*! So *truck* needs a *u*, right there in the middle!"

"Super job, editors! If the word isn't in the room somewhere, you can still work on it by saying it slowly and hearing more sounds!" I congratulated them. "I bet you are ready to tackle your own writing!"

LINK

Send students off, reminding them to edit their writing by rereading and making sure their words look right.

"So, Super Writers, today is your last day to make changes! If you have things you need to do, you can start with that. Or you can make changes to your words, too, just like we did in our piece about reading in the library with Mr. Kolk. Start by looking again at the writing you will be publishing at our celebration tomorrow. Reread it as if it were your independent reading book; read it with your finger, just like we did together, and check to make sure your words look right. If you see a word that doesn't look right, rewrite it above so that it *does* look right. Try to fix up as much as you can today. From now on, you can always do this work when you get your writing ready to share with an audience."

At this, I sent them off to make their final editing decisions.

Supporting Students as Editors

AS YOU WORK WITH YOUR STUDENTS TODAY, remember that your goal for them is not to have every word perfectly spelled, but rather to have fixed up a few words so that their writing is more legible. Writers will do their best, which won't be the same for every child. In the previous sessions, much of children's spelling work was done as they composed. Now, you are teaching them to spell as they edit.

Some of your students may feel overwhelmed because they know there are many misspellings in their writing. One strategy to help kids with this feeling is to have them focus on a certain number of words. You might say, "Read your writing and circle five words you think you can write even better and with more power because you have learned so much more about how to write words." Then, help these students

MID-WORKSHOP TEACHING   Fancying Up Writing for an Audience

"Writers, before you can read your pieces at the author's celebration, you need to make them the best they can be.

"Today you're going to do this by going back to your pictures to make sure that as you add color, you really think hard about making the colors clarify your writing!

"So, I want you to think about this before you start. First, read your piece to yourself. Then, talk to a friend about how you might use the colored pencils today to help your reader understand what is important in your story or teaching book." There was a quiet hum in the classroom as children read their pieces to themselves. Once students began talking, I walked around, listening to different partnerships discuss how to best add color.

"Writers, before you get started, listen to what some of your friends are saying they will do today. Annie is going to color in her cat, because her cat is the most important part, and Annie wants her to show up! She is going to make sure that she colors in her cat the same way on each page. Daniel is going to color in people's faces and especially the slanted eyebrows on his sister's face so that readers know how angry she is in his story.

"So, writers, for the rest of writing time and from now on, do what writers do and fancy up your pieces with the details, or colors, that pop out what's important. Work slowly and carefully so that you make your books even more beautiful. Tomorrow is the big day!"

As Students Continue Working . . .

"Super Writers, make sure you are rereading your writing. Let me hear you reading. Point underneath each word."

"Slide your finger under the words and listen to the sounds. Say the word slowly and think about what letters might be missing. Then, write them in!"

"Don't forget, you can use the words in the room to help you find another spelling for some of your words."

"If you finished your story, go on to another story. See what you can edit in that one."

rewrite an entire word from scratch or add onto the existing letters that are there. Taking on the remaining words will now feel less challenging.

You might work with kids individually or in small groups to identify words to add or fix up. You might suggest word wall (or high-frequency) words, such as *the*, *a*, *and*, and *my*. These words also help build the concept of word and one-to-one match, and help make parts more memorable. If it hasn't come up yet, now is the perfect time to make sure everyone knows that the word *I* is always capitalized.

Some children will want to apply their new knowledge of sight words to all the pieces in their folders. Gabriela chose to work not only on her piece for the celebration, but also on other pieces she liked (see Figures 18–2 and 18–3). These pieces show how Gabriela spent her time fixing up her words by adding the high-frequency words she had learned.

You may find it helpful to create a group by putting two partnerships together to work on editing and spelling. You have taught partnerships to rehearse and plan stories together and to give each other tips for elaboration and revision. Now, you can add to their repertoire by teaching them how partners can figure out words together. Partners can also reread their work with the Narrative Writing Checklist in hand.

Since this is the second-to-last session in this unit of study, you'll certainly want to use your own checklist to help you think about what your children have and have not learned to do. Pay attention to the big things: their engagement in writing, their understanding of why people write, their abilities, their proclivity to work productively with stamina and independence, and their progress as they've moved toward writing coherent detailed texts and toward recording their content using the conventions of written language.

FIG. 18–2 Gabriela's writing: *My mom put me to sleep at night. My puppy slept with me.* (Labels: *The sun. The door. Me. Mom. My puppy.*) Notice how Gabriela has added some high-frequency words to make two-word lables.

FIG. 18–3 *One sunny day, me, my mom, and brother drove to me cousin's house.* (Labels: *The car. My brother. Mom. Me. House. Sun. Clouds.*) Here, you can see how the writer worked again on words like *clouds*, *brother*, and *house* and also added in a few high-frequency words to make two-word labels.

Reflecting on Growth

Invite the children to share their writing with others and see what their classmates have done.

"Writers, when you come to the meeting area, bring the writing that you will be celebrating tomorrow. You will see a piece of writing from the very first day of school on your rug spot. Put your new writing on top of that one and just sit on both of those pieces, please."

Once all the children had convened, I began. "Writers, when I was growing up, my mother stuck a decal of a giraffe onto the back of one of our doors. This wasn't just any ol' giraffe. It was a giraffe *measuring stick*. On each birthday, I had to stand as tall as possible against it, heels up against the wall, and then my mother would figure out my height and write my name and the date at that place on the measuring stick. All these years later, I can look at the markings on that giraffe and think, 'Wow. I was once *that* little? Then I grew *that* much?'

"I'm telling you this because tomorrow's celebration will be like a writer's birthday. It will mark a unit of your writing life. And so this is a good time to notice how much you have grown. The best way to do that is to look between the first piece of writing you made this year and the story you just published, and to think, 'How have I changed?'

"Will you and your partner show each other what your writing was like at the very start of this year and what it has been like more recently, and talk about how you have changed as a writer?" I listened in as children talked about their work. Many seemed amazed at the differences between the two pieces.

"I used to just scribble and now I take my time and draw for real."

"This piece doesn't have any words. And now I have *lots* of words."

"I make books now. I don't just make one page and then I am done."

"I know how to write my name. Look at this first one. My name isn't right!"

"I can't even remember what I was writing the first day of school. I didn't even know what to do. Now I know what to do."

Today, you will bring back the teaching books students created in the first part of this unit. It probably seems like months ago that you clipped all that work together, emptying their folders to make room for stories. You may want to use all of the clipped-together writing or just the very first piece from the first day of this unit. Have this bundle (or piece) waiting for them at the meeting area or tables, depending on where you want them to do the work of this share session.

This activity can last a while, generating a long list of ways students have grown. The point is to give children an awareness of and pride in the great distance they have come as writers, to drum up enthusiasm and momentum to continue that growth trajectory in the coming unit.

Reading into the Circle
An Author's Celebration

$\mathcal{D}$ear Teachers,

I will never forget the day my first book, *Lessons from a Child* (1983), arrived in the mail. I remember hearing the Federal Express truck drive up to the house and thinking, "This is it." I remember tearing the box open and sitting there, my book in my hands, thinking, "I'm an author. I wrote this. My book, by me."

That single moment changed my life. From that moment on, I have been a writer. My life is infinitely more interesting to me because I'm in the business of spinning it into stories and mining it for insights. More than anything, I want children to learn that they, too, are writers and that they can take the true details of their lives and put them on the page in ways that will make people gasp and laugh and listen intently and want to hear more. The day that does the most to teach children that they are writers is the day we celebrate children's published work.

Here are a few guidelines to follow in planning your celebration. First, remember that you'll have several of these across the year. Don't make the occasion lavish and exhausting. The celebrations will grow in scale and complexity, so keep this first publication simple. Try to design a celebration that reflects the purposes of the unit. A unit on revision will celebrate drafts. An author study might end with children writing "about the author" pages for their own books. The purpose of this unit has been to launch your children into a life of writing, and your celebration needs to highlight the fact that each and every child is now an author. You will want to celebrate the children in your classroom, their stories, and their newfound identities as writers.

Ideally, celebrations not only highlight your main goals for the unit but also emphasize the importance of reading and sharing your work with an audience. While the celebration may feel like a fun time without much instructional purpose, children are actually learning a lot about how to present their ideas and knowledge. This is just as vital a part of the writing process as storytelling or drafting. As writers, children will come to expect that their writing is for an audience, made of real-life people who will read and comment on the writing. This helps them write with more clarity and detail and usually more energy. When it is time to share and hear the reactions of others, children realize the power and impact their words can have. In the earliest celebrations you will probably need to help your students read and listen to one another's books—books that will now be added to the bookshelves of your classroom. You will want to make a big deal about all the new stories that you now have in your classroom and how similar they are to the books in your library.

Having children read whole stories for the class can take a long time, and those who are not reading may stop listening by the fourth or fifth story. One way to approach this is to have a two-part reading. Each child can read a single page into the circle of classmates, and then they can all break into groups of four or five to share their entire pieces. When all the stories have been read and enjoyed, you might make a toast to their amazing growth and let them spend some time drinking juice and talking over the event.

What follows is a description of one celebration to give you an image of how one might go.

Good luck!

Lucy and Amanda

BEFORE THE CELEBRATION

Before this day, children can practice how the celebration will go. They can practice how this Reading into the Circle will go, from forming a circle with their bodies to reading with a strong voice and listening well. They should have their favorite parts of their writing ready and rehearsed. Children learn that when they are finished reading, they must turn to the person on the right so that the next person knows when to begin reading. They can also practice forming their small groups and going off to their special place or table in the room where they will read to each other.

To make sure the day had a special feel from the moment the children walked in, I stood near the door as they came into the room in the morning, to be sure to greet each and every one with a special message. "Good morning, Super Writers. What a special day today is. Our classroom looks kind of different today. We all came ready for something super special. I even got all dressed up!" There was a different feeling in the air on this cool September morning. Students were a bit more dressed up, a bit more excited. "Today's our celebration," Gabriela said. "I couldn't sleep last night! I was so excited."

"I know," I concurred. "It's going to be great! I thought about it the whole time I was exercising in the gym this morning! On a special day, like today, our workshop will be a little different. We won't write today." The children all looked at each other with a bewildered look on their face. "I know that seems strange. Today, Super Writers, we are going to *read* and *listen* to one another! We are going to hear *many* stories from *many new authors!*

"I have chosen some of our favorite authors and stories to read today! I have also fixed up my writing and our class story that we can share. And remember, after we Read into the Circle, each one of you will go off with a few friends where you will get a chance to read your whole piece of writing." I pointed to a chart with each student listed under a group number. "In case you have forgotten which group you are in, I have all the groups listed here on our classroom chart."

"When we share our writing we use our best voices as readers and our best eyes and ears as listeners. First, we are going to come to our meeting area and make a big circle! Then we are each going to get a chance to read our favorite line or part into the circle! When the reader is reading, where do all our eyes and ears turn to?" I gave a slight pause. The students' eyes were fixed on me, waiting with anticipation. So I lowered my voice, to have them lean in even closer, and I whispered, "The reader. All of our eyes and ears should be on the reader. Are you ready?"

Everyone nodded. "Show me that you are ready to start this celebration! Take your writing in your hand and sit up—just like a writer. Show me which writers are ready to come to our celebration of Reading into the Circle! Wow, everyone really looks like a writer who is ready to read and share."

THE CELEBRATION

"It is time for our author's celebration," I announced. "Writers, let's gather." I steeped my voice with excitement and raised my hands slowly, indicating it was time for everyone to stand up and walk slowly to the meeting area. The students stood up with a little bit of apprehension but instead of calling them again to the meeting area or telling them to hurry, I just waved my hands, encouraging them to form a circle. Their writing was in their laps.

"Welcome to our first writing celebration. I am so proud of all that you have done in writing workshop. You have learned to draw pictures and write words about the things that matter to you. You have also learned that if you get to a hard part, you just do the best you can. You have learned how to choose a piece of writing and revise and edit it. You did a great job. You should give yourselves a round of applause." They all clapped.

"Writers, let's start Reading into the Circle with Casey." Casey picked up her piece of writing (see Figure 19–1), already open to her favorite page, and read, "And they were twirling around and laughing and telling jokes." Some of the students giggled, remembering the rest of Casey's story.

As she soaked up the giggles, Casey turned her head to the right. Deja knew this was her signal to start, so she picked up her piece of writing (see Figure 19–2), turned to her favorite page, and read, "Then my dog pooped in his bed." Everyone giggled again, remembering how Deja was trying to clean up her room when her dog had an accident! Then Deja looked to her right, and Annie read just her title page, "Book." Then she turned to her right, to the next reader. This continued until every child in the class had an opportunity to Read into the Circle.

As the last reader finished sharing his or her favorite part, I held several beats of silence to allow the words in the air to sink in. "Now, with that as the appetizer, we can move to our tables, hear the whole pieces from the people in our groups, and share our own writing! So group 1, will you stand up?" On cue, a small group of writers stood up. "You all can read your writing in the back corner. Group 2, you may go to the art area. Group 3, you may go near the writing center, and group 4, stay right here."

FIG. 19–1 Casey's favorite page: *And they were twirling around and laughing and telling jokes.*

I try not to say a word from the time the Reading into the Circle starts until the time it ends. This adds to the magic of the ritual and lets the students feel the power of the writing. When there is no talking save for the reading of the words of writers, and the reading goes from one student to the next smoothly, the words shimmer in the air and students can feel the suspense of waiting for the next reader to begin.

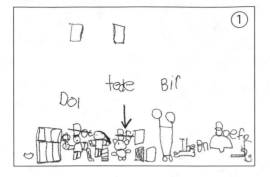

FIG. 19–2   Deja's writing: *First what happened. It was messy, my room. Then I put my toys away.* (Labels: *Doll. Teddy Bear. The bone. Bed for my dog.*)

I took my book and put it on the shelf. Then my dog pooped in his bed. (Labels: *Windows. The bed.*)

I had to clean it up with a wipey. Oh no! I took care of my dog. (Labels: *The Bed. Toys. Windows.*)

I gave my dog love. (Labels: *Me. Dog. Heart.*)

As I walked around the room, I stopped occasionally to make sure everyone was listening to the person reading, and to solve minor problems, but mostly I was in the background, simply reveling in all that these children had accomplished.

"Stop, look, and listen." I sang out.

"Oh yeah!" they all replied.

"Wonderful reading, Super Writers. It looks like most of you have finished reading and are ready for the next part of our celebration. Can I draw your attention to the bulletin board we have over here in our classroom? Will you read it with me please? It says, "We Are All Writers!" Isn't that true! Right below the board, I have some baskets, with our favorite stories in them—stories we have been reading again and again since the first day of school! I am going to hang *your* writing right above these baskets of favorite stories! It will be an extension of our library!

①

②

③

FIG. 19–3   Evelyn's writing: *Mom and me were going to meet a friend.*

My friend met us at the street. We did not know..

I love seeing my friend. She is nice.

④

⑤

Finally I spin it. (Labels: My friend. Me. Rope. Speech bubble: I see you.)

We love to see my friend.

"Before we have refreshments, I thought we could gather back in the meeting area. On your way over, please drop your writing off by the bulletin board, into one of the baskets with our other favorite stories. Then come on over and I will reread some of our favorite stories so far this year!"

I read our class story first. Then we moved on and read, *Creak! Said the Bed*. I read a couple of favorite parts from a few other stories.

When we had finished reading our books, it was time for the final phase of the celebration. "Writers, are you ready to have refreshments?" Amid the chorus of "Yeahs," I stood up and headed over to our refreshment table. The students' eyes followed me. I looked over to the class and said, "Come join me at the refreshment table for a quick toast. Groups 1 and 2, stand up and come over to the table and make a circle."

As the students hurried to the table, I handed each of them a cup of juice in a brightly colored cup. "You have to wait for the toast," I cautioned, as I handed out the juice. "Don't drink it yet."

FIG. 19–4   Natalie's writing: *Celebration by Natalie.*

We got our books. (Label: Celebration)

We lined up to go to the library.

We went up the stairs. (Labels: Let's read. So cool.)

We read our books.

Then we went back to class. (Labels: Me.)

Once each child had a cup of juice, I said. "I would like to make a toast (that means I am about to say some really nice things). Writers, you have worked hard. You deserve this very special day. May we continue to have writing celebrations that are as terrific as this one. Congratulations!"

AFTER THE CELEBRATION

After the celebration, remind students about the long, hard work they did in the writing workshop. Many teachers make a bulletin board with students after the celebration, entitled something like, "We Are Writers." This board holds a finished piece of writing from each student next to a photograph of him or her. Some teachers add quotations from children about writing and about themselves as writers.

"'I like to write long stories about my grandmother.'—Carl"

"'When you think you can't write another word, just get a drink of water and ideas just *pop* into your head!'—Khadija"

"'When we have writing workshop, we can hear pencils scratching all over the place.'—Talia"

Some teachers end the unit by creating a wall with a square for each child to fill with artifacts or pictures that say something about themselves as writers. Children then have a chance to talk with each other about what their artifacts and pictures say about their writing lives. Other teachers create a space for children to post writing questions and tips that support each other as a community of writers. These various ways of celebrating help students see themselves as writers, which motivates them to learn even more about the things that writers do. However you decide to invite your students to reflect on and display their work, you will have a lasting artifact to refer to as you start your next unit of study.

FIG. 19–5   Johanna's writing, "Pumpkins"

Papa and me went to a pumpkin patch. We drove in a car.

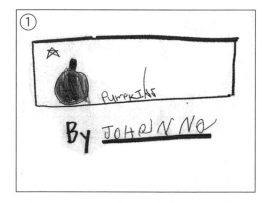

We saw lots of pumpkins. Big ones and small ones. (Labels: *Papa. Me.*)

We found a big one and put it on the car. (Label: *Pumpkin.*)